E ÁTHA CLIAT'I THEAS

LAW *of* CONNECTION

ALSO BY MICHAEL J. LOSIER

Law of Attraction

LAW *OF* CONNECTION

MICHAEL J. LOSIER

HODDER

MOBIUS

First published in Great Britain in 2009 by
Hodder Mobius
An imprint of Hodder & Stoughton
An Hachette UK company

1

A CIP catalogue record for this title is
available from the British Library

Hardback ISBN 978 0 340 97891 7
Paperback ISBN 978 0 340 97892 4

Typeset by Hewer Text UK Ltd, Edinburgh
Printed and bound in Great Britain by Clays Ltd, St Ives plc

Hodder & Stoughton policy is to use papers that are natural,
renewable and recyclable products and made from wood grown in
sustainable forests. The logging and manufacturing processes are
expected to conform to the environmental regulations of the
country of origin.

Hodder and Stoughton
338 Euston Road
London NW1 3BH

www.hodder.co.uk

Contents

PART I. THE 3 CONDITIONS FOR CONNECTING

PART II. NLP COMMUNICATION STYLE SELF-ASSESSMENT

PART III. THE 4 NLP COMMUNICATION STYLES

PART IV. CALIBRATING YOUR CONVERSATIONS

Why I Wrote This Book

After the publication of my first book, *Law of Attraction*, I heard from thousands of people who told me how much it had helped them to identify and draw in more of what they truly wanted in their personal and business relationships.

But these people also wanted more. They wanted to know how they could better communicate with and feel understood by *all* the people they came in contact with, both personally and professionally. That's what made me realize I had to write *Law of Connection* to give them the skills they needed to create rapport with all kinds of people on a daily basis.

Both *Law of Attraction* and *Law of Connection* are about mastering a few simple rules that will help you to lead a fuller, richer, more meaningful life. You don't need to have read one to benefit from the other. Each law stands on its own. And each offers its own rewards.

For all the years I've been teaching the Law of Attraction, I've incorporated the information you're about to learn into my training seminars, interviews, and coaching in order to connect with audiences, interviewers, reporters, talk-show hosts, and all the people I interact with every day.

One of the compliments I appreciate receiving the most is that I am able to make complicated ideas easy to learn. I owe that ability to my training in Neuro-Linguistic Programming (NLP) and the use of Accelerate Learning Techniques (ALT). These techniques are designed to appeal to every communication style. For example:

- ◆ Some of you will enjoy the white space in the book, while others won't.
- ◆ Some of you will enjoy the illustrations, while others will not even notice them.
- ◆ Some of you will like the summaries or worksheets or the case studies.

I've incorporated these techniques into this book so that everyone will be able to learn from it easily and enjoyably.

My intention is that most of you will refer to *Law of Connection* time and time again to remind yourselves of the words and scripts you can listen for or use to communicate better in all kinds of situations.

You might even catch yourself putting a little tab in YOUR communication style section for quick, easy reference.

I hope that you will enjoy this book's simplicity, share it with your family, introduce it in your workplace, and discover how communication improves wherever you are.

Michael Losier
www.LawofConnectionBook.com

MICHAEL LOSIER

How This Book Will Improve Your Relationships

If not you, then someone you know probably spends a lot of time complaining about relationship conflicts. We're hearing it everywhere: at home, at work, and in our communities.

Conflict is everywhere, between:

Married couples
Dating couples
Parents and children
Teachers and students
Office workers
Management and staff
Business to business

This book will give you all the information and techniques you need to improve your communication and build better, healthier relationships.

Sometimes changing only a few words can make all the difference; sometimes it's more than a few words. But whatever the nature of the negative or conflicted relationship, this book will help.

The process and techniques will seem simple, and you may catch yourself saying, "It can't be this easy," or "This is too simple to make a difference." If you find yourself thinking these thoughts, just remember, the results will speak for themselves.

Since 1999, I have been teaching couples, trainers, teachers, coaches, counselors, and all kinds of people in all kinds of relationships the key to successful communication—and now I'll be teaching it to you.

Have fun with the information. Watch and listen as your connections with others improve and conflict is eliminated.

MICHAEL LOSIER

How to Use This Book

This book can be read in a few hours or less. Before you do anything else, read it through from cover to cover so you get the big picture and a better understanding of the process.

Then read it again, this time completing the Communication Style Self-Assessment and the worksheets. Doing that will help you to understand and internalize the information as you begin to apply it to your everyday life.

Also, invite and encourage your family to complete the Communication Style Self-Assessment. You will see and hear how much fun it is to apply what you learn about each other's communication style.

Make this book and material a family affair. Incorporate it at the workplace.

As you master the information, you will likely find yourself teaching others how they, too, can improve their communication skills and enhance their relationships.

Additional self-assessments and worksheets are available online at www.LawofConnectionBook.com.

Why Is the Law of Connection a Law?

Most people can recall a situation when they either were or were not connecting with another person.

The Law of Connection states that when two people are in rapport they will have a better connection.

The reason it's called a law is because it follows one simple rule.

> The Rule: The more rapport you have with somebody, the stronger your connection with that person. The less rapport you have with someone (or when the rapport is broken) the weaker your connection is with that person.

Your rapport, and therefore your connection, is the result of how you communicate.

This book will help you understand your communication style, its gifts, and its challenges. And, more important, it will help you to understand other people's styles, their gifts, and their challenges, so that, through observation and practice, you become a more flexible communicator who can connect with people of all styles.

The key to connection is becoming a more flexible communicator. Flexibility is the requirement. If you go to France you will communicate better if you are able to speak French. Being flexible in your communication will help you connect with others quickly and easily.

PART I

THE 3 CONDITIONS FOR CONNECTING

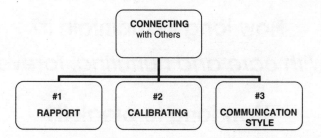

RAPPORT

How long to build it?

Sometimes seconds and some-times years.

How long to maintain it?

With care and nurturing, forever.

How long to break it?

Only seconds.

How long to repair it?

Sometimes never.

Rapport—Condition 1

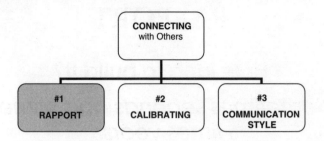

Many of us can recall a time when we have met someone we instantly liked—or someone we instantly disliked, despite having something in common with that person.

> **rap·port**, noun
> relationship; esp., a close or sympathetic relationship; agreement; harmony

Building rapport with a person can happen instantly or it can take a while to develop.

Rapport is a key part of communication. Communication happens on two levels—verbal and nonverbal.

There are two common ways most people either fail to achieve or break rapport with others: by not picking up on verbal and nonverbal cues to the other person's communication style, and through miscommunication, because one person doesn't understand the other's style. *Law of Connection* will give you all the tools you need to achieve, and not break, rapport.

Calibrating—Condition 2

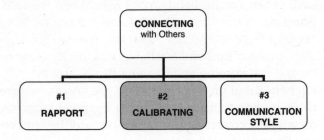

Calibrating is the art of paying attention and responding to what you've noticed. It's about picking up on the verbal and nonverbal cues (such as laughing, blushing, nail-biting, or stammering) that indicate another person's mental or emotional state and then adjusting your own communication style to match or accommodate theirs. By calibrating, you build rapport.

When you don't pay attention, you could end up making assumptions or jumping to conclusions without really knowing what the other person is thinking or feeling. When you fail to calibrate your style to theirs, you could end up breaking rapport.

People who are good calibrators are able to quickly assess a situation and respond to it in a way that establishes and maintains rapport. As a result, other people find it easy to have them around. Not being able to calibrate is annoying and frustrating to others and causes misunderstandings that break rapport.

Here are three examples of how calibrating works.

MICHAEL LOSIER

Coming home from work:

A working couple arrives home within thirty minutes of each other. The husband arrives first. When the wife gets home she is bursting with excitement about having received a huge promotion. However, she notices immediately that her husband is still wearing his jacket and tie and is slamming and banging things around in the kitchen. Based on those two cues, she knows that something is wrong. Instead of sharing her good news immediately, she creates rapport by going into the kitchen to greet him, express her concern, and ask how he's doing.

Serving diners in a restaurant:

Two friends having dinner together are in the middle of a serious conversation when their overly cheerful server bounds up and, without paying any attention to the mood at the table, announces with a big smile, "Hi there, I'm Biff, I'll be your server tonight!" The server hasn't noticed the seriousness of the diners' mood and has failed to calibrate his style to theirs—thereby sabotaging himself by failing to build the rapport he had intended to create.

Entering a library vs. a cafeteria:

As a loud group of teenagers leaves the noisy cafeteria and enters the library, they immediately calibrate and adjust the volume of their conversation to match the quiet of the library. This establishes rapport with everyone who is already working quietly in the room.

Very often you have only nonverbal cues to help you calibrate another person's mental or emotional state. Here are a number of nonverbal cues you can watch out for to help increase your calibrating skills.

Examples of Nonverbal Cues That Indicate Mood

Blushing	Turning pale	Blue lips
Gasping for air	Rapid breathing	Shallow breathing
Giggling	Pacing the floor	Sweating
Laughing	Wringing hands	Biting fingernails
Whispering	Upright posture	Slouched over
Stammering	Staying silent	Repeatedly checking time
Smiling	Frowning	Wiggling

You will no doubt have many opportunities to observe nonverbal cues at work, in your primary relationship, and with your entire family. Now that you are aware of these cues, you will certainly notice when others have not calibrated well. You will come to see and understand the direct link between calibrating well and increasing rapport—as well as how failing to calibrate breaks the connection.

MICHAEL LOSIER

Understanding Communication Styles—Condition 3

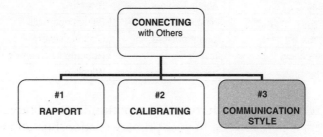

The third condition for creating connection, understanding others' communication styles, is so important that I have devoted fully one-third of this book to teaching you how to do it.

Your ability to understand and match another person's communication style is what will make you a good calibrator and keep you in rapport so that there is a good connection between you. Not understanding someone else's style is quite often the reason two people are not connecting.

The four communication styles are Visual, Auditory, Kinesthetic, and Digital.

Whether you are communicating with a group or an individual, understanding each of the four communication styles will help you stay in rapport and connection.

In Part III I'll be helping you to learn and understand more about each of these styles, but first I'm going to ask you to complete the ten-question self-assessment on the following pages. Don't overthink it; just answer the questions quickly and intuitively.

PART II

NLP COMMUNICATION STYLE SELF-ASSESSMENT

The Self-Assessment Questionn...

On a scale of 1 to 4	Sample Question:
4 = *Closest to describing you*	I make important decisions based on:
3 = *Next closest description*	Sample Answer:
2 = *Somewhat describes you*	<u>4</u> My gut feeling and comfort level
1 = *Least descriptive of you*	<u>1</u> How the idea sounds to me
	<u>3</u> How it looks to me
	<u>2</u> Precise review/study of the issues

1. **I make important decisions based on:**

    ___ My gut feeling and comfort level

    ___ How the idea sounds to me

    ___ How it looks to me

    ___ Precise review and study of the issues

2. **During a disagreement, I am most likely to be influenced by:**

    ___ The volume and tone of the other person's voice

    ___ Whether or not I can see the other person's point of view

    ___ The logic and rationale of the other person's opinion

    ___ Whether or not the other person is sensitive to my feelings

3. **When communicating with others, what's important to me is:**

    ___ The way I dress and look

    ___ Sharing my feelings and experiences

    ___ Knowing that the meaning of my words is understood

    ___ Being heard and listened to

4. **When someone is asking me an important question, I tend to:**

___ Listen carefully, then ask questions to ensure I understand

___ Prefer time to think it over and to choose my words carefully

___ Appreciate being given time to search inside for the answer

___ Answer quickly, describing it in pictures

5. **I would consider myself:**

___ Attuned to the sounds of my surroundings

___ Able to easily make sense of new facts and data

___ Sensitive and flexible in my relationships

___ Creative and able to handle tremendous amounts of information quickly

6. **People really know me best when they:**

___ Can relate to what I'm feeling

___ Can see my perspective

___ Listen carefully to what I have to say and how it is said

___ Are interested in the meaning of what I am communicating

7. **When working on a project with others, I am more likely to:**

___ Want to improve the process with my ideas

___ Want to be part of the vision and planning process

___ Want to sequence the events and put things in order

___ Want to help build good solid relationships

8. When describing things to me:

___ Showing it to me brings clarity

___ I can remember well just by listening

___ Writing it down helps me to integrate it

___ Presenting the facts in a logical way makes sense

9. In times of stress, I am most challenged with:

___ Trusting people, situations, or concepts

___ Being diplomatic, being too blunt and to the point

___ Separating my feelings from what other people are feeling

___ Being flexible and changing the timing of plans

10. I find it easy and natural to:

___ Receive inner inspirations

___ Tell where new ideas fit in

___ Follow the direction of tried-and-true methods

___ Organize and plan events

Your Self-Assessment Summary Worksheet

Step 1:

Copy your answers to each question from the Self-Assessment Questionnaire onto the lines below. See sample.

1.	Sample Question
	I make important decisions based on: (On a scale of 1 to 4)
__4__ **K**	My gut feeling and comfort level
__1__ **A**	How the idea sounds to me
__3__ **V**	How it looks to me
__2__ **D**	Precise review/study of the issues

1.	2.	3.	4.	5.
____ K	____ A	____ V	____ A	____ A
____ A	____ V	____ K	____ D	____ D
____ V	____ D	____ D	____ K	____ K
____ D	____ K	____ A	____ V	____ V

6.	7.	8.	9.	10.
____ K	____ A	____ V	____ D	____ D
____ V	____ V	____ A	____ A	____ A
____ A	____ D	____ K	____ K	____ K
____ D	____ K	____ D	____ V	____ V

MICHAEL LOSIER

Your Communication Processing Style Score Sheet

Going from left to right, copy the numbers for each question from the Summary Worksheet into the box **under** the corresponding letter on the score sheet below. See the sample for how to do this.

Question	V	A	K	D	Total
Sample	3 2	1 9	4 1	2 3	10
1	2	9	1	3	10
2	4	3	2	4	10
3	1	4	2	3	10
4	1	2	9	3	10
5	1	2	3	4	10
6	1	4	3	2	10
7	2	1	4	3	10
8	3	2	1	4	10
9	3	4	1	2	10
10	1	3	4	2	10
Total	19				100

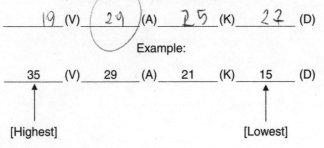

My Communication Processing Order is:

__19__ (V) __29__ (A) __25__ (K) __27__ (D)

Example:

__35__ (V) __29__ (A) __21__ (K) __15__ (D)

↑   ↑

[Highest]   [Lowest]

Understanding Your Score Results

Your **Highest Score** represents your dominant or preferred style of communicating with others and interpreting incoming information.

Your **Lowest Score** represents your weakest or least preferred style of communicating with others and interpreting incoming information.

A **Tied Score** indicates you have a high preference for two or more communication styles. As you learn about each communication style in the next section of this book, you will discover which of them you tend to favor or use most often.

Even a 1-point difference in scores is enough to determine your dominant or preferred style.

Understanding Your Relationships with Others

You may find it helpful to record your scores, and as you encourage your family, close friends, and workmates to read this book, ask them to enter their scores as well.

This reference chart will show you whose communication styles are most similar to yours and whose are opposite to yours. This will give you an opportunity to individualize your communications and therefore create better connections with everyone you know.

Communication Styles Reference Chart

Ideally, you can print or copy this chart and refer to it as you learn more about the communication styles of others in your life.

Name	Highest	Lower	Lower	Lowest
Sample	V	K	D	A

You can download additional copies of the Communication Styles Reference Chart at www.LawofConnectionBook.com.

Once You Know Your Scores, Then What?

Have you noticed that when you meet certain people you just don't seem to have any rapport? You say one thing; they hear something different. You simply don't understand one another.

When you feel an immediate rapport with someone, it means you are matching their communication style—thus, making a connection. When you don't have that rapport, it is probably because you have different communication styles, and therefore each of you is misinterpreting what the other is saying, thinking, or feeling.

It is HIGHLY likely that there are people in your life whose communication style is different from yours.

Do all your family members have the same communication style? Probably not—which is another reason to have your family members share what's in this book. Imagine what it would be like if each of you knew and understood how the others liked to receive information. I can assure you, it would make for a happier home.

What about people in business? Do all your customers and clients communicate the same way you do? No, they don't. A salesperson's ability to calibrate AND understand his customer's/client's communication style is important for making a good connection and a sale.

In Part III I'll be explaining in detail how each of the four communication styles prefers to operate.

PART III

THE 4 NLP
<u>COMMUNICATION STYLES</u>

Why Recognizing Your Own and Other People's Communication Styles Matters

Once you recognize your own communication style you will understand why you state things or ask questions in a particular way.

Understanding other people's styles allows you to see why they receive and communicate information the way that they do.

Having that information will allow you to be flexible and calibrate your communication style so that you create rapport and improve your connections with all different types of communicators.

In the following pages I'll be introducing you to four different characters, each of whom exhibits the behaviors of a particular communication style.

Through them you will become more aware of your own communication strengths and weaknesses and learn why it is that you connect well with some people and why you may NOT be connecting well with others.

More important, you will learn how to adjust your communication style to create more rapport in all your relationships.

Having this information is extremely important in all areas of your life because:

♦ Your communication style may be different from that of your partner or spouse.
♦ A mother of four children may find that each child has a different communication style.

- ♦ Your friends may have different communication styles that either do or do not match your own.
- ♦ A manager or supervisor could have employees with all four styles.
- ♦ A teacher could have students with all four styles.
- ♦ Salespeople may have clients with all four styles.

As we proceed I'll be using the following graphics to remind you which style we're discussing in each of the sections below.

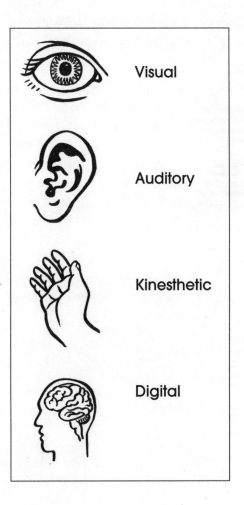

Visual

Auditory

Kinesthetic

Digital

The Visual Communicator

Meet Visual Vicky

Vicky's highest score on the self-assessment is Visual.

If your HIGHEST score is Visual you will likely be able to relate to Vicky and her characteristics. She processes information and communicates the same way you do.

If Visual was your LOWEST score, you will want to pay attention to Vicky's style, as this may be the type of communicator with whom you have the least connection.

In the following pages you will learn more about Visual communicators so you can figure out the best way to connect with them.

Common Characteristics of the Visual Style

If you are a Visual Style communicator, you will no doubt recognize these qualities in yourself. If you're not, once you understand how Visual Style people operate—how they learn and process information best—you will be able to connect with them much faster and easier.

Visual Style People

♦ See things as pictures
♦ Memorize by creating visual pictures in their mind
♦ Learn quickly
♦ Get bored easily when they have no plans
♦ Value time, so they like things to start and end punctually
♦ Prefer getting the "big picture" rather than the details

How Often Do You Use These Words?

Here is a list of words Visual communicators commonly use. If you are a Visual Style communicator, these words will be very familiar to you. If you are not, they may seem foreign to you.

In the boxes below, indicate with a ✔ whether you use each of these words rarely or often.

	Rarely	Often
Focus		
Imagine		
Look		
See		
Show		
Visualize		
Illustrate		
Clear/clearly		
Clarify		
Picture		
Bright		
Appear		
Dull/hazy		
View/scan		
Enlighten		

What Did You Learn or Become More Aware of as a Result of Completing This Exercise?

Example: I realized how rarely I use these words.

Example: I use these words all the time. I wonder if I'm using them too often?

_____

_____

_____

_____

_____

_____

_____

_____

To build rapport and connect with Visual Style communicators, you need to be aware of the words they use and prefer to hear most often. And if you are a Visual Style communicator, you also need to be aware of how often you use these words. Having that awareness will make you a more flexible communicator and will enhance your connections with people whose styles are different from your own.

Commonly Used Phrases for the Visual Style Communicator

In addition to listening for Visual Style communicators' commonly used words, you can also observe and listen for the phrases they most often use in their expressions, greetings, and goodbyes.

Visual Style Commonly Used Expressions

• I **see** what you mean.	• I want to get a **new perspective**.
• That's not **clear** enough.	• I get the **picture**.
• Don't keep me in the **dark**.	• I **see** what you are talking about.
• This is making me **see red**.	• That's **fuzzy** to me.
• Just give me the **big picture**.	• Can you **clarify**?

Visual Style Commonly Used Greetings and Goodbyes

Greetings	Goodbyes
• It's great to **see** you.	• **See** you later.
• You are **looking** great.	• I'll **look** for you online.
• I've been **looking** forward to it.	• **See** you around.
	• **See** you soon.

Gifts and Challenges of the Visual Style Communicator

It is important to understand that each communication style comes with gifts and challenges. If you are a Visual Style communicator, you need to know what others say they *like* about this style (gifts) and what others are often *challenged* by.

What Others LIKE about Visual Style Communicators

♦ They can move from one subject to another at lightning speed.
♦ They are good at understanding the "big picture" or "vision" and running with it.
♦ They are great time managers.
♦ They are good at coming up with "big picture" or "future vision" ideas.

Other characteristics and behaviors of the Visual Style communicator can, however, be challenging to others.

By being more aware of these challenges and learning how to manage them, you will bring more flexibility to your communication style and connect better with people whose style is different from yours.

What Others Find CHALLENGING about Visual Style Communicators

♦ They become rigid and inflexible when faced with timing or scheduling changes.
♦ They become impatient with listening to or reading details.
♦ They tend to skip over details.
♦ They can be impatient with others.
♦ They tend to rush others and themselves.

How to Build and Stay in Rapport with the Visual Style Communicator

Most of us have been in situations where we've broken rapport with someone or where someone has broken rapport with us, so we know how negative that feels. In effect, it breaks the connection between us. The better the rapport you have with someone, the greater your connection with that individual will be.

If you are not a Visual Style communicator, it is important to know what will build or break rapport with someone who is.

Because Visual Style people value TIME so highly, you will build or break rapport with them by doing the following:

Builds Rapport	Breaks Rapport
Providing an agenda	Changing appointments without giving them time to change the plan they've pictured in their mind
Keeping meetings/sessions short	
Honoring start and end times	Telling long stories with too many details
Giving plenty of notice when changing, postponing, or rescheduling events	Holding long meetings
	Arriving late for a scheduled meeting
Getting to the point quickly when conversing	Asking them for detailed information
	Leaving long voice-mails or sending long e-mails

When the Visual Style Person Is Stressed or Out of Balance

We have all seen situations where people are stressed, anxious, or just not themselves. It is as though their life is temporarily out of balance.

Below is a list of situations that are likely to stress Visual Style people, along with the behaviors they are likely to exhibit. If you are a Visual Style person, you will recognize these behaviors in yourself. If you see them in another person, it's a good bet that he or she is a Visual Style communicator.

What Causes the Visual Style Person to Become Stressed or Out of Balance?

◆ They can become rigid and inflexible if the picture in their head gets changed too fast or too often.
◆ They become impatient with too many words, details, and nonstop talking.
◆ They can become irritated if projects/tasks are not done on time or if someone is late for a social engagement.

If you are aware of what causes Visual Style people to become stressed and out of balance, there are things you can do to alleviate the stress and help them get back in balance. If you are a Visual Style person, you can use these tactics to calm yourself and regain your own balance.

How to Help the Visual Style Person Get Back in Balance

◆ Give them plenty of notice when making a change to their schedule. In a personal relationship this might mean giving your date or your partner advance notice when you're going to be later than you'd planned. In business it might mean trying not to reschedule a meeting at the last minute.
◆ Keep your information short and clear. Whether you're planning a social activity or a business meeting, just state the time and place. Don't give more details than the Visual Style person needs or wants.

- Suggest they take time to organize and tidy their room or their workspace.
- Suggest they plan a future project or activity, whether it's a vacation or a new business plan.

How to Ask Questions That Stimulate Answers from the Visual Style Communicator

You know you are matching another person's communication style and making a connection when he or she answers your questions quickly and easily. Using words or phrases the other person can relate to is one way to create that connection.

Here is a list of questions that stimulate quick responses from the Visual Style communicator.

Questions That Stimulate Answers

- Do you **see** what I mean?
- **Look** okay?
- Tell me what your **picture looks** like.
- How does this **look** to you?
- Are you getting the **picture**?
- Is this **clear**?

Now that You Understand the Visual Style . . .

Take an inventory of the people in your personal and business life. Who in your life do you think processes information in the Visual Style? On the following worksheet, enter the person's name in Column A. In Column B indicate the reasons why you suspect or know that he or she processes information visually. In Column C indicate, by writing "yes" or "no," whether you think your connection with this person is good or whether it could use some improvement.

A	B	C
Name	Why I Think They Process Visually	Good Connection? Yes / No
Victor	Likes short meetings, uses many visual words, talks in big picture	No

If you wrote "no" in Column C for any of these people, indicate below what you have learned you can do to improve that relationship.

I will reduce the details when talking to Victor.
I will remember to use more visual words.

The Auditory Communicator

Meet Auditory Allan

Allan's highest score on the self-assessment is Auditory.

If your HIGHEST score is Auditory, you will likely be able to relate to Allan and his characteristics. He processes information and communicates the same way you do.

If Auditory was your LOWEST score, you will want to pay attention to Allan's style, as this may be this type of communicator with whom you have the least connection.

In the following pages you will learn more about the Auditory communicators so you can figure out the best way to connect with them.

Common Characteristics of the Auditory Style

If you are an Auditory Style communicator, you will no doubt recognize these qualities in yourself. If you're not, once you understand how Auditory Style people operate—how they learn and process information best—you will be able to connect with them much faster and easier.

Auditory Style People

♦ Remember what they hear—word for word
♦ Learn by listening and often don't take notes
♦ Are good storytellers
♦ Talk to themselves when working or concentrating (You can often hear them making sounds like ahh, hmmm, oooh, umm)

How Often Do You Use These Words?

Here is a list of words Auditory communicators commonly use. If you are an Auditory Style communicator, these words will be very familiar to you. If you are not, they may seem foreign to you.

In the boxes below, indicate with a ✔ whether you use each of these words rarely or often.

	Rarely	Often
Resonate		
Harmony		
Repeat		
Tune in		
Buzz		
Discuss		
Ringing		
Listen		
Sound		
Noisy		
Whisper		
Tune		
Hear/heard		
Say		
Babble		
Clicking		
Quiet		
Earshot		

What Did You Learn or Become More Aware of as a Result of Completing This Exercise?

Example: I realized how rarely I use these words.

Example: I use these words all the time. I wonder if I'm using them too often?

_____

_____

_____

_____

_____

_____

_____

_____

To build rapport and connect with Auditory Style communicators, you need to be aware of the words they use and prefer to hear most often. And if you are an Auditory Style communicator, you also need to be aware of how often you use these words. Having that awareness will make you a more flexible communicator and will enhance your connections with people whose styles are different from your own.

Commonly Used Phrases of the Auditory Style Communicator

In addition to listening for Auditory Style communicators' commonly used words, you can also observe and listen for the phrases they most often use in their expressions, greetings, and goodbyes.

Auditory Style Commonly Used Expressions

• **Tell me** more.	• **Squeal** like a pig.
• I **hear** you **loud** and clear.	• **Tune** in/out.
• That **rings** a **bell**.	• That **clicks** for me.
• It was **music** to my **ears**.	• That **resonates** with me.
• It was all **double talk**.	

Auditory Style Commonly Used Greetings and Goodbyes

Greetings	Goodbyes
• I'm glad you **called** to **chat**.	• I'll **talk** to you later.
• So good to **talk** to you.	• **Call** later.
• I **called** to **tell** you…	• **Chat** later.

Gifts and Challenges of the Auditory Style Communicator

It is important to know that each communication style comes with gifts and challenges. If you are an Auditory Style communicator you need to know what others say they *like* about this style (gifts) and what others are often *challenged* by.

What Others LIKE about Auditory Style Communicators

- ◆ They are frequently eloquent speakers.
- ◆ They are "ideas" people (great for brainstorming).
- ◆ They love discussions and give lengthy descriptions or explanations.
- ◆ Many are great writers and editors.
- ◆ They are great storytellers.

♦ They like to make improvements (on both things and processes).

Other characteristics of the Auditory Style communicator can, however, be challenging to others.

By being more aware of these challenges and learning how to manage them, you will bring more flexibility to your communication style and connect better with people whose style is different from yours.

What Others Find CHALLENGING about Auditory Style Communicators

♦ They tend to be blunt, harsh, or seem too direct.
♦ Being diplomatic is a challenge for them.
♦ They give strong opinions whether solicited or not.
♦ They are quick to anger if they feel they are not being heard.
♦ When angry they will argue to make their point and blame others.
♦ They often interrupt and have a hard time letting others finish their sentences.
♦ They tend to jump from subject to subject.
♦ They may sulk or withdraw when their ideas are not accepted.
♦ They may fall in love with the sound of their own voice.
♦ They will repeat themselves until they are convinced they are being heard.

How to Build and Stay in Rapport with the Auditory Style Communicator

Most of us have been in situations where we've broken rapport with someone or where someone has broken rapport with us, so we know how negative that feels. In effect, it breaks the connection between us. The better the rapport you have with someone, the greater your connection with that individual will be.

If you are not an Auditory Style communicator, it is important to know what will build or break rapport with someone who is.

Because Auditory Style people value FAIRNESS the most, you will build or break rapport with them by doing the following:

Builds Rapport	Breaks Rapport
Asking them about themselves	Doing something else while they are speaking to you (they will feel unheard)
Avoiding pressuring them	
Helping them stick to the subject	
Listening closely	Interrupting them too often
Breaking things down into small steps and then helping them prioritize	Raising your voice when you speak to them
	Speaking with a harsh tone
Repeating things back to them	Rushing them when they are telling a story
Telling them you hear them ("I heard you," or "I hear what you are saying")	Using words sloppily or misspelling
	Having background noise that they cannot turn off
	Using audio material that is of poor quality either technically or grammatically

When the Auditory Style Person Is Stressed or Out of Balance

We have all seen situations where people are stressed, anxious, or just not themselves. It is as though their life is temporarily out of balance.

Below is a list of situations that are likely to stress Auditory Style people, along with the behaviors they are likely to exhibit. If you are an Auditory Style person, you will recognize these behaviors in yourself. If you see them in another person, it's a good bet that he or she is an Auditory Style communicator.

What Causes the Auditory Style Person to Become Stressed or Out of Balance?

♦ They withdraw and can be frustrated when their ideas are challenged or rejected.
♦ They may raise their voice if they feel they are not being heard.
♦ They go from participating in a dialogue to giving a long-winded lecture.

If you are aware of what causes Auditory Style people to become stressed and out of balance, there are things you can do to alleviate the stress and help them get back in balance. If you are an Auditory Style person, you can use these tactics to calm yourself and regain your own balance.

How to Help the Auditory Style Person Get Back in Balance

♦ Let them know you are open to their input and ideas.
♦ Tell them you will be their sounding board for a specific period of time.
♦ Be totally present as a listener, and give them your full attention.
♦ If they wander from the subject or carry on too long, gently nudge them back on track.
♦ Help them to focus on exactly what it is they really want.

How to Ask Questions That Stimulate Answers from the Auditory Style Communicator

You know you are matching another person's communication style and making a connection when he or she answers your questions quickly and easily. Using words or phrases the other person can relate to is one way to create that connection.

Here is a list of questions that stimulate quick responses from the Auditory Style communicator.

Questions That Stimulate Answers

- ◆ How does this **sound**?
- ◆ **Tell** me . . .
- ◆ Are we in **tune** with each other?
- ◆ What's your **idea**?
- ◆ Does this **ring a bell**?
- ◆ How can this be **improved**?
- ◆ Does this **click** with you?
- ◆ **Sound** good?
- ◆ Does this **resonate** with you?

Now That You Understand the Auditory Style . . .

Take an inventory of people in your personal and business life. Who in your life do you think processes information in the Auditory Style? On the following worksheet, enter the person's name in Column A. In Column B indicate the reasons why you suspect or know that he or she is an auditory processor. In Column C indicate, by writing "yes" or "no," whether you think your connection with this person is good or whether it could use some improvement.

A	B	C
Name	Auditory	Good Connection? Yes / No
Allan	*Likes to talk—a lot. He is great at giving ideas and loves to tell stories.*	*No*

If you wrote "no" in Column C for any of these people, indicate below what you have learned you can do to improve that relationship.

I can ask him how to improve something, thus allowing him to have a "voice."

Really listen and acknowledge him by saying "I hear you."

The Kinesthetic Communicator

Meet Kinesthetic Kelly

Kelly's highest score on the self-assessment is Kinesthetic.

If your HIGHEST score is Kinesthetic you will likely be able to relate to Kelly and her characteristics. She processes information and communicates the same way you do.

If Kinesthetic was your LOWEST score, you will want to pay attention to Kelly's style, as this may be the type of communicator with whom you have the least connection.

In the following pages you will learn more about Kinesthetic communicators so you can figure out the best way to communicate with them.

Common Characteristics of the Kinesthetic Style

If you are a Kinesthetic Style communicator, you will no doubt recognize these qualities in yourself. If you're not, once you understand how Kinesthetic Style people operate—how they learn and process information best—you will be able to connect with them much faster and easier.

Kinesthetic Style People

♦ Often speak slowly
♦ Learn best through doing
♦ Need time to "feel their way" through new information
♦ May say that they "feel" something is either right or wrong when asked to make a decision
♦ Have a tendency to take time to "settle into" a new environment or situation or to nest

How Often Do You Use These Words?

Here is a list of words Kinesthetic communicators commonly use. If you are a Kinesthetic Style communicator, these words will be very familiar to you. If you are not, they may seem foreign to you.

In the boxes below, indicate with a ✔ whether you use each of these words rarely or often.

	Rarely	Often
Feel		
Firm		
Together		
Relationship		
Touch		
Connect		
Press		
Catch		
Hard		
Complete		
Fun		
Soft		
Play		
Numb		
Stumble		
Fit		
Strike		
Comfortable		
Grasp/Handle		

What Did You Learn or Become More Aware of as a Result of Completing This Exercise?

Example: I realized how rarely I use these words.

Example: I use these words all the time. I wonder if I'm using them too often?

_____

_____

_____

_____

_____

_____

To build rapport and connect with Kinesthetic Style communicators, you need to be aware of the words they use and prefer to hear most often. And if you are a Kinesthetic Style communicator, you also need to be aware of how often you use these words. Having that awareness will make you a more flexible communicator and will enhance your connections with people whose styles are different from your own.

Commonly Used Phrases for the Kinesthetic Style Communicator

In addition to listening for Kinesthetic Style communicators' commonly used words, you can also observe and listen for the phrases they most often use in their expressions, greetings, and goodbyes.

Kinesthetic Style Commonly Used Expressions

• Let's **touch** upon this.	• It **feels** right to me.
• Get **comfortable** with…	• I'm getting a **grasp** on this.
• **Walk** me through this.	• I've got a **handle** on that now.
• It just **rubs** me the wrong way.	• This **fits**.
• I get the **point**.	• That **sits** well with me.

Kinesthetic Style Commonly Used Greetings and Goodbyes

Greetings	Goodbyes
• I **love** it when you call.	• Take **care**.
• I'm **happy** to hear from you.	• **Hugs**.
• I'm **excited** you called.	• Nice **connecting** with you.
• Let's **catch** up.	• Let's **connect** soon.
• **Feels** good to **connect** again.	• Stay in **touch**.

Gifts and Challenges of the Kinesthetic Style Communicator

It is important to understand that each communication style comes with gifts and challenges. If you are a Kinesthetic Style communicator, you need to know what others say they *like* about this style (gifts) and what others are often *challenged* by.

What Others LIKE about Kinesthetic Style Communicators

- They are good at relationship building.
- They are extremely loyal.
- They are nurturing and supportive.
- They are detail oriented.
- They are great team players.

Other characteristics and behaviors of the Kinesthetic Style communicator can, however, be challenging to others.

By being more aware of these challenges and learning how to manage them, you will bring more flexibility to your communication style and connect better with people whose style is different from yours.

What Others Find CHALLENGING about Kinesthetic Style Communicators

- Most have challenges making decisions quickly.
- They can get overwhelmed when presented with too many choices.
- They tend to provide more details than most people need or want.
- They can be slow and methodical and therefore take more time than others to complete a task.
- They may be needy and therefore "high-maintenance" in both personal and business relationships.

How to Build and Stay in Rapport with the Kinesthetic Style Communicator

Most of us have been in situations where we've broken rapport with someone or where someone has broken rapport with us, so we know how negative that feels. In effect, it breaks the connection between us. The better the rapport you have with someone, the greater your connection with that individual will be.

If you are not a Kinesthetic Style communicator, it is important to know what will build or break rapport with someone who is.

Because Kinesthetic Style people tend to value RELATION-SHIPS and CONNECTIONS so highly, you will build or break rapport by doing the following:

Builds Rapport	Breaks Rapport
Providing an agenda for both personal and business meetings or events	Feeling excluded
Making it a point to connect with them in group situations so they feel included	Being interrupted or "talked over"
	Overwhelming them with too many ideas or choices at once
Being sensitive to their need to be comfortable in their physical environment	Disregarding their intuitive and emotional reactions or contributions to a plan or project
Providing start and end times/dates for all events and projects	Stopping the fun and stifling their creativity by overanalyzing
Allowing them time for creativity, fun, play, and socializing	
Offering them a few clear, simple choices	

When the Kinesthetic Style Person Is Stressed or Out of Balance

We have all seen situations where people are stressed, anxious, or just not themselves. It is as though their life is temporarily out of balance.

Below is a list of situations that are likely to stress Kinesthetic Style people, along with the behaviors they are likely to exhibit. If you are a Kinesthetic Style person, you will recognize these behaviors in yourself. If you see them in another person, it's a good bet that he or she is a Kinesthetic Style communicator.

What Causes the Kinesthetic Style Person to Become Stressed or Out of Balance?

- ♦ They feel hurt when they sense that they are being excluded or left out.
- ♦ When they don't feel comfortable or confident in a situation or a relationship they can be needy and demanding of attention.
- ♦ When they feel negativity in a situation or relationship they may withdraw and want to escape, both physically and emotionally.
- ♦ When they have too many choices or complicated tasks to complete they may become overwhelmed and avoid doing what needs to be done.
- ♦ They will do almost anything to avoid conflict and tend to become passive instead of standing up for themselves or voicing an opinion.

If you are aware of what causes Kinesthetic Style people to become stressed and out of balance, there are things you can do to alleviate the stress and help them get back in balance. If you are a Kinesthetic Style person, you can use these tactics to calm yourself and regain your own balance.

How to Help the Kinesthetic Style Person Get Back in Balance

- ◆ Ask them how you can best support them.
- ◆ Give them time to be alone in their own space.
- ◆ Encourage them to separate their own feelings from those of other people.
- ◆ Give them the guidance they need to take action and keep moving forward.
- ◆ Don't overwhelm them with too much information at once. Break projects down into small steps and give them "start dates" in advance.
- ◆ Offer to become their "support person" and offer to do things with them as a team.
- ◆ Listen patiently, and give them lots of time to get to the point.

How to Ask Questions That Stimulate Answers from the Kinesthetic Style Communicator

You know you are matching another person's communication style and making a connection when he or she answers your questions quickly and easily. Using words or phrases the other person can relate to is one way to create that connection.

Here is a list of questions that stimulate quick responses from the Kinesthetic Style Communicator.

Questions That Stimulate Answers

- ◆ How does this **feel**?
- ◆ What would make this more **comfortable** for you?
- ◆ Does this **fit** for you?
- ◆ Can you **relate** to this?
- ◆ Do you feel **complete** with this?
- ◆ Does this **work** for you?

Now That You Understand the Kinesthetic Style . . .

Take an inventory of the people in your personal and business life. Who in your life do you think processes information in the Kinesthetic Style? On the following worksheet, enter the person's name in Column A. In Column B indicate the reasons why you suspect or know that he or she processes information kinesthetically. In Column C indicate, by writing "yes" or "no," whether you think your connection with this person is good or whether it could use some improvement.

A	B	C
Name	Kinesthetic	Good Connection? Yes / No
Karen	*She takes a lot of time to answer my questions and can become overwhelmed if I rush her.*	*No*

If you wrote "no" in Column C what can you do to improve that relationship?

Give her time to "feel through" the questions I ask her.

Build more connection with her before we start to talk business.

Use more feeling words when we chat.

Take the time to share or give a hug.

_____

_____

_____

_____

_____

_____

_____

_____

MICHAEL LOSIER

The Digital Communicator

Meet Digital Dan

Dan's highest score on the self-assessment is Digital.

If your HIGHEST score is Digital, you will likely be able to relate to Dan and his characteristics. He processes information and communicates the same way you do.

If Digital was your lowest score, you will want to pay attention to Dan's style, as this may be the type of communicator with whom you have the least connection.

In the following pages you will learn more about Digital communicators so you can figure out the best way to connect with them.

Common Characteristics of the Digital Style

If you are a Digital Style communicator, you will no doubt recognize these qualities in yourself. If you're not, once you understand how Digital Style people operate—how they learn and process information best—you will be able to connect with them much faster and easier.

Digital Style People

♦ Memorize by steps and sequences
♦ Process information in a methodical, rational, and logical way
♦ Are very detail oriented
♦ Have a strong need to make sense of the world around them
♦ Learn by working things out in their mind
♦ Need time to process new information

How Often Do You Use These Words?

Here is a list of words Digital communicators commonly use. If you are a Digital Style communicator, these words will be very familiar to you. If you are not, they may seem foreign to you.

In the boxes below, indicate with a ✔ whether you use each of these words rarely or often.

	Rarely	Often
Perceive		
Consider		
Detail		
Know		
Describe		
Figure out		
Process		
Logical		
Conceive		
Change		
Sequence		
First/Last		
Think		
Thought		
Rational		
Decide		
Understand		

What Did You Learn or Become More Aware of as a Result of Completing This Exercise?

Example: I realized how rarely I use these words.

Example: I use these words all the time. I wonder if I'm using them too often?

_____

_____

_____

_____

_____

_____

_____

To build rapport and connect with Digital Style communicators, you need to be aware of the words they use and prefer to hear most often. And if you are a Digital Style communicator, you also need to be aware of how often you use these words. Having that awareness will make you a more flexible communicator and will enhance your connections with people whose styles are different from your own.

Commonly Used Phrases for the Digital Style Communicator

In addition to listening for Digital Style communicators' commonly used words, you can also observe and listen for the phrases they most often use in their expressions, greetings, and goodbyes.

Digital Style Commonly Used Expressions

• Without a **doubt**.	• **Make sense** of it.
• **Word** for **word**.	• Pay **attention** to . . .
• **Describe** in **detail**.	• I **know**.
• **Figure** it out.	• I **know** what you **mean**.

Digital Style Commonly Used Greetings and Goodbyes

Greetings	Goodbyes
• Hello.	• Bye for now.
• Yes . . .	• Bye.
• This is John . . .	

Gifts and Challenges of the Digital Style Communicator

It is important to understand that each communication style comes with gifts and challenges. If you are a Digital Style communicator you need to know what others say they *like* about this style (gifts) and what others are often *challenged* by.

What Others LIKE about Digital Style Communicators

- They are good at solving complex problems.
- They are great strategists.
- They are excellent at sequencing and structuring tasks and projects.
- They manage details extremely well.
- They are extremely adept at planning events, parties, or outings.
- They see how the parts fit together to create the "big picture."
- They are fiercely loyal.

What Others Find CHALLENGING about Digital Style Communicators

- They are slow to trust new people, new things, and even new concepts.
- They hate being interrupted.
- They can be stubborn and like to be asked to do something instead of being told what to do.
- They don't volunteer information and need to be asked specifically.

How to Build and Stay in Rapport with the Digital Style Communicator

Most of us have been in situations where we've broken rapport with someone or where someone has broken rapport with us, so we know how negative that feels. In effect, it breaks the connection between us. The better the rapport you have with someone, the greater your connection with that individual will be.

If you are not a Digital Style communicator, it is important to know what will build or break rapport with someone who is.

Because Digital Style people value KNOWING about their future so highly, you will build or break rapport with them by doing the following:

Builds Rapport	Breaks Rapport
Providing an agenda	Barging into their private space
Creating timelines with them	Expecting an immediate response to questions you've sprung on them while they are focused on something else
Allowing them time for closure and completion	
Using logic and providing facts and figures when making decisions	Presenting too many new ideas and not giving them time to process details
Providing a quiet and private work environment	Telling them what to do rather than asking and/or giving them choices
Giving them sufficient preparation	Taking their contributions for granted and forgetting to acknowledge them
Showing that you trust them	Changing the agenda without including them in the process

When the Digital Style Person Is Stressed or Out of Balance

We have all seen situations where people are stressed, anxious, or just not themselves. It is as though their life is temporarily out of balance.

Below is a list of situations that are likely to stress Digital Style people, along with the behaviors they are likely to exhibit. If you are a Digital Style person, you will recognize these behaviors in yourself. If you see them in another person, it's a good bet that he or she is a Digital Style communicator.

What Causes the Digital Style Person to Become Stressed or Out of Balance?

- ◆ When their schedule is interrupted or their routine is disrupted, they tend to become rigid and stubborn.
- ◆ When their sense of order is disrupted, they try to restore it themselves without regard for other people's needs or feelings.
- ◆ When they are stressed they withdraw from communication.
- ◆ They can become stressed about things that *might* happen sometime in the future.

If you are aware of what causes Digital Style people to become stressed and out of balance, there are things you can do to alleviate the stress and help them get back in balance. If you are a Digital Style person, you can use these tactics to calm yourself and regain your own balance.

How to Help the Digital Style Person Get Back in Balance

- ◆ Ask them what they need to make something better.
- ◆ Give them time alone to think things through.

- ◆ Encourage them to eat, because they often forget to eat when deeply involved in a project.
- ◆ Remind them to trust the present process, and encourage them not to worry so much about the future.

How to Ask Questions That Stimulate Answers from the Digital Style Communicator

You know you are matching another person's communication style and making a connection when he or she answers your questions quickly and easily. Using words or phrases the other person can relate to is one way to create that connection.

Here is a list of questions that stimulate quick responses from the Digital Style communicator.

Questions That Stimulate Answers

- ◆ What do you **think** this **means**?
- ◆ Do you **understand**?
- ◆ Is this **making sense**?
- ◆ Can you **make sense** of this?
- ◆ What do you **think**?
- ◆ What are your **thoughts** on this?
- ◆ Can you **describe** it in **detail**?

Now That You Understand the Digital Style . . .

Take an inventory of the people in your personal and business life. Who in your life do you think processes information digitally? On the following worksheet, enter the person's name in Column A. In Column B indicate the reasons why you suspect or know that he or she processes information digitally. In Column C indicate, by writing "yes" or "no," whether you think your connection with this person is good or whether it could use some improvement.

A	B	C
Name	Digital	Good Connection? Yes / No
David	Always wants lots of details and tends to need time to process my questions.	Yes
Abigail	Hates it when she's working on the computer and I interrupt her train of thought.	No

If you wrote "no" in Column C, what can you do to improve that relationship?

I'll try not to interrupt Abigail when she's in the middle of something and schedule times for us to talk so that she can plan in advance.

PART IV

CALIBRATING YOUR CONVERSATIONS

Calibrate in Order to Connect

Now that you've taken the self-test and read about the four communication styles, you should be aware of your own preferred method of receiving and processing information. And you may have also discovered which style is the least familiar or natural to you.

You probably have said:

♦ "This is so me; I say this all the time."
♦ "This resonates with me."
♦ "These are my behaviors exactly."

And you may have said this about your least dominant style:

♦ "I never use these words."
♦ "These words sound foreign to me."
♦ "These kinds of people drive me crazy."

 ## Meet Expert Edward

Edward knows the four communication styles well and is always willing to help his friends with their miscommunication problems.

In the following conversations you will see how and why people who have different styles can find it difficult to build rapport, and how calibrating your style to match that of the person with whom you are trying to connect can change a negative dynamic into a positive one.

Once you've "listened in" to these real-world conversations, it will be much easier for you to put what you've learned about the four communication styles to work in every aspect of your own life. We all need and/or want to make connections every day, in business situations and personal relationships. Whether you're a manager trying to solicit the cooperation of a colleague on a project, a parent explaining something to a child, a teacher communicating with a student, or someone seeking to create a deeper, more meaningful personal relationship, you'll find that your ability to calibrate will make all your communications more effective and more positive.

What's important to remember is that just because you're a Visual or Auditory or Kinesthetic or Digital communicator, it doesn't mean you can't build rapport and make significant connections with people of different styles. You absolutely can, and becoming aware of how to calibrate your own style to theirs is what's going to help you do that.

Here are four case studies that show you why there was a breakdown in communication and how it was easily corrected by understanding the other's communication style.

Visual Vicky Wants to Make a Sale

Visual Vicky is a store clerk working in the TV department. She notices a customer checking the manual on one of the display models and taking notes. Vicky, being Visual, assumes the customer likes the looks of the TV, so she approaches and says, "Hi, may I show you the TV? The picture you get on this large screen is really great."

Customer:	[Pauses for a moment] Hmmm, no thanks. I'm just collecting information right now.
Visual Vicky:	Let me show you how it looks.
Customer:	What's the warranty? I actually want to start there.
Visual Vicky:	Sure. I'll just turn it on first so you can see the quality of the picture.
Customer:	Well, I'd rather have my questions on the warranty answered first. [Continuing in an abrupt tone of voice] I'd like to shop on my own. When I have questions I'll come and talk to you.

The customer never did come back to Visual Vicky. He continued taking notes and then left the store.

Visual Vicky feels that she's been dismissed, and she knows that she's broken rapport with the customer.

Later that evening she calls her friend Expert Edward. She tells him what happened and asks for his advice.

 First, Expert Edward tells Visual Vicky that he can tell the customer was likely a Digital Style communicator because of his focus on details and his organized note-taking.

Expert Edward points out the characteristics and words the customer used:

♦ Checking the manual
♦ Collecting information and taking notes
♦ Asking "What's the warranty?"

- Saying he wanted to "start there"
- Stating that he would let her know "when I have questions"

Then Edward explains to Visual Vicky that she had been using Visual words and phrases that caused her to break rapport with her Digital customer. Now Visual Vicky can really understand the causes of their inability to connect.

Expert Edward also recommends what she could do differently the next time she serves a Digital customer:

- Give him time to collect more information before approaching him.
- Ask him what he thinks of a particular model.
- Ask him, "Can I tell you more about the warranty?"
- Give him longer to process the information he's collected and make a decision.
- Invite him to come to her when he has more questions.

If Vicky's customer had been an Auditory Style person, he might have:

- Asked her how the sound was
- Asked her to tell him more about the different sets
- Told a long story about problems he'd had with another TV

She could have:

- Asked him how each of the sets "resonated" with him
- Asked him, "How does this one sound?"
- Led him back to the subject when he wandered off the point

If Vicky's customer had been a Kinesthetic Style person, he might have:

♦ Asked her personal questions to try to connect with her more
♦ Asked for some time to get a "feel" for the different TVs on display
♦ Told Vicky he'd "reconnect" with her after he got "comfortable" with the choices

And she could have:

♦ Asked what he "felt" he wanted from his new TV
♦ Suggested he get more familiar with either this one or that one (thereby reducing his number of choices)
♦ Said she'd leave him alone to get a better "feel" for the sets and checked back with him in ten minutes

• •

Teaching point: Expert Edward gives Visual Vicky an assignment. He suggests that in the staff room, or beside the cash register, she should keep a quick reference guide of the four styles and their behaviors. Within a short period of time she'll be able to recognize a customer's style and calibrate her response without referring to the guide. She'll have integrated the information, and it will be second nature to her. He also suggests that Visual Vicky share this guide with all of the staff.

• •

Auditory Allan Breaks Rapport with His Girlfriend

Auditory Allan finds he has to keep repeating stuff to his girlfriend, and he doesn't understand why she's always accusing him of changing the subject. It also seems to him that some of the things he says hurt her feelings, and he doesn't know why.

Recently, Allan and his girlfriend had an argument because she said he'd agreed to do something—his exact words were "that sounds like a good idea"—and then, when the time came, he denied that he'd ever agreed to do it. According to him, he was just commenting on how the idea sounded, not agreeing to do it.

Finally, even though Allan tells her all the time what he likes about her, she wants to be touched and held, and she says that he doesn't make her feel special.

Auditory Allan: I want to tell you about this great idea I have for a new project.

Girlfriend: Another idea? What happened to the last idea you came up with? You never did anything about that.

Auditory Allan: I don't feel that you're hearing me. I want to tell you all about it.

Girlfriend: Go ahead. But I feel like you never stick to one thing. You're all over the place.

Auditory Allan: It sounds like you don't care about what's important to me.

Girlfriend: I didn't say that.

Allan knows just the person to call—his friend Expert Edward. Edward will tell him what's going wrong with this relationship.

When Allan explains the problems he and his girlfriend have been having, Edward points out that some of his classic Auditory Style traits are getting in the way of their building rapport—particularly since it seems that Allan's girlfriend is a Kinesthetic communicator:

♦ You have a lot of ideas and you want to share them, but you keep changing your focus.
♦ When you say that something sounds like a good idea, your girlfriend thinks you mean that you're agreeing to do it. Then when you don't do it, she's disappointed and her feelings are hurt.
♦ Your Kinesthetic girlfriend wants you to be more demonstrative with your feelings rather than just telling her what you feel.
♦ You can be very blunt, and your tone of voice can be brusque, and she's sensitive to what you sound like, not just to your actual words.

Edward then suggests how Allan might build more rapport with his girlfriend in the future:

♦ When she makes a suggestion, say "yes, I want to" or "no, I don't want to" in order to avoid any confusion.
♦ Instead of *telling* her how you feel, try *showing* her by touching her or holding her.
♦ Ask her what you can do to make her more comfortable.

If Allan's girlfriend were a Visual Style communicator, she might have:

- Told him to just give her the "big picture" instead of boring her with all the details of his idea
- Told him, "I don't 'see' why you said it was a good idea if you didn't mean it. You were just wasting my time."

And Allan could have:

- Built rapport by telling her how beautiful she looks
- Kept his explanations short and sweet instead of rambling on about every detail that pops into his head
- Made sure that when he makes a plan he sticks to it and shows up on time

If Allan's girlfriend were a Digital Style communicator, she might have:

- Asked him what steps he was going to take to implement his plan
- Asked him for some time to think about what he'd suggested
- Worried about what might happen if this or that about the plan went wrong

And Allan could have:

- Presented his ideas logically and asked her if they made sense
- Built rapport by not interrupting her when she was speaking
- If she became unnaturally quiet, asked her what she needed to decide if the idea worked for her

Teaching point: Edward suggested that Allan make a list of the ways he could either create or break rapport with his Kinesthetic Style girlfriend and carry it with him until they became automatic for him. Edward also reminded Allan that the more he practiced using the words and behaviors that create connection with Kinesthetic Style communicators, the less he would have to consult his cheat sheet.

Kinesthetic Kelly Connects with a Coworker

Kinesthetic Kelly feels very disconnected because her coworker never wants to go for lunch or coffee, and she worries that the coworker doesn't like her. Meanwhile, her coworker is frustrated because the projects they're working on together always seem to take more time than they should to complete.

Kinesthetic Kelly: I'd like to get together for lunch so that we can talk about how our project is coming along.

Coworker: I had planned on doing four or five errands during my lunch hour. What exactly do you want to discuss?

Kinesthetic Kelly: Oh, I just wanted to connect with you and touch base.

Coworker: Truthfully, I like it when we have an agenda so I know what we're going to talk about and how long it's going to take. Can we set up a half-hour meeting at two o'clock when we both get back from lunch?

Kinesthetic Kelly: Yes, we can. I am also hoping to hear how things are going with you.

Later that evening, Kelly calls Expert Edward, relays the conversation, and confides her feelings to him. Edward says, "I'm not surprised to hear that you're having some difficulties. I know that you process kinesthetically, and your communication style can be challenging to people who communicate differently. Edward reminds her of some of the characteristics of a Kinesthetic Style communicator:

♦ Relationships are important to you.
♦ You like to socialize.
♦ You like to chat about personal stuff without getting down to work.
♦ You like to have a good connection with people.
♦ You like to get to know your coworkers.
♦ You give too much detail.
♦ You always want to do things with your coworkers outside of office hours.
♦ You always want to have face-to-face meetings.

"It's not that your coworker doesn't like you," Edward reminds her, "but my hunch is that he's a Visual Style communicator." Edward knows this because:

♦ He wanted to know what was on Kelly's agenda.
♦ He wanted to keep their meeting short and to the point.
♦ He wanted a specific time frame for the meeting.
♦ He didn't want to mix business with socializing.

Edward then suggests phrases Kelly might use in the future to create more rapport with her Visual Style coworker:

♦ I just wanted to get a better picture of how things were going.

- ♦ I've been looking forward to setting up a meeting with you.
- ♦ I know you're busy, so we'll keep it short.
- ♦ I don't need all the details. Just give me the big picture.

If Kelly's coworker had been an Auditory Style communicator, he might have:

- ♦ Given her a long, rambling explanation of why he couldn't have lunch with her
- ♦ Interrupted her explanation of why she wanted to have the lunch
- ♦ Been too blunt in voicing his refusal

And Kelly could have:

- ♦ Asked him to tell her more about the projects he was working on (which would also make Kelly comfortable, since she likes to create personal connections)
- ♦ Made sure to give him her full attention when they were speaking
- ♦ Gently guided him to keep him on track if he started to ramble

If Kelly's coworker had been a Digital Style communicator, he might have:

- ♦ Asked her for a lot of details about why she wanted to have lunch with him
- ♦ Told her he would have to figure out how to fit it into his schedule
- ♦ Asked her to lay out a plan for their conversation

And she could have:

- ◆ Created rapport by telling him there was a project she thought he could manage
- ◆ Assured him that she trusted his judgment and whatever he decided would be OK
- ◆ Given him time to think about his answer to her request

• •

Teaching point: To help her identify her coworkers' communication styles, Expert Edward asks Kelly to create a spreadsheet with the names of all her coworkers along with their most commonly used words and phrases and their typical behaviors. He suggests that she keep it in a folder on her desk where she can refer to it easily until she gets a better handle on everyone's style, which will lead to her creating good relationships with all of them.

• •

Digital Dan Helps His Child with Her Homework

Digital Dan is trying to help his child complete her homework, but he becomes totally frustrated because she refuses to stick with the orderly agenda he's laid out.

Digital Dan: [Turning off the radio that's been playing in the background.] You've got to stick to this homework schedule.

Child: That method doesn't resonate with me. I like to do a little of this and a little of that. It doesn't have to be done in order. [Child turns music back on.]

Digital Dan: You can't possibly concentrate with all of this music on.

Child: It sounds good to me. I can hardly hear it. It doesn't distract me at all.

Digital Dan: [Grumbling] That just doesn't make sense to me. How can you even think with all of that noise?

Child: You're not listening to me. I told you it doesn't bother me.

The fact that his daughter is "all over the place" and never seems to finish what she starts drives Dan crazy. He leaves the room in total frustration.

Once again, the daughter and Dan have created some negativity in the room, and the daughter doesn't feel heard.

That evening, Dan calls Expert Edward for help. He asks Edward what he can do to make his daughter more like him. He wants her to approach her homework in an orderly fashion. After Dan repeats their earlier conversation word for word, Expert Edward tells Dan that his daughter is an Auditory Style communicator and explains how he came to that conclusion:

♦ She had the radio on in the background.
♦ She told him he wasn't listening to her.
♦ She has trouble focusing, preferring to jump from one subject to another.

Edward then explains that because he is a Digital Style communicator he wants his daughter to do everything in sequence, in an order that seems logical to him. But that isn't going to work for her because her style is different from his.

Expert Edward then gives Dan a list of questions he can ask his daughter to help them to communicate better and build more rapport the next time he helps with her homework:

♦ Does this sound okay?
♦ How does this sound to you?
♦ Does this ring a bell?
♦ Is this clicking?
♦ What are your ideas?

• •

Teaching point: Expert Edward suggests that Dan keep the list of questions in his wallet, like a pocket guide, until he masters his daughter's style—which he will probably do very quickly.

• •

If Dan's daughter were a Visual Style communicator, she might have:

- ◆ Told him he was wasting her time with all that talking
- ◆ Said, "I don't 'see' why you need to tell me all this"
- ◆ Said, "Just give me the big picture and leave me alone so that I can get it done"
- ◆ Said she would "show" him what she'd done when it was finished

And he could have:

- ◆ Created rapport by asking to "see" what she'd been doing
- ◆ Said, "This 'looks' good to me"
- ◆ Told her he'd be back in an hour to "see" how things were going—and made sure to be on time

If Dan's daughter were a Kinesthetic Style communicator, she might have:

- ◆ Said, "I have a good 'feel' for my English assignment, but I'm not so 'comfortable' with the math"
- ◆ Asked him if they could do the assignment together as a team
- ◆ Asked him how he had "felt" about homework when he was in school

And he could have:

- Asked how he could best "support" her in getting it done
- Told her they could make it a "team effort"
- Helped her to break down the math problems into small steps so that she wouldn't become overwhelmed

PART V

THE 4 EASY METHODS YOU CAN USE TO MAKE BETTER CONNECTIONS

Reframing, Future Pacing, Installing, and Positive Presupposition

Reframing, Future Pacing, Installing, and Positive Presupposition are four easy methods anyone can master in order to communicate more effectively and therefore create better connections in all kinds of everyday situations.

The way we view our own past, present, and future—as well as the way we can persuade others to view theirs—can make the difference between creating and breaking rapport. The more positively we see and talk about things, the more positive our communications will be. The more positively we communicate, the better we connect, and the more likely we are to receive a positive response.

Incorporating the following methods into your daily communications will help to ensure that you are connecting better with others in every aspect of your life.

Reframing

What it is:

When you reframe something you are looking at it from a different point of view. Reframing is a way to turn what might be viewed as a negative scenario into a positive one.

What it does:

When you change the meaning of an event you can change a potentially negative communication into a positive one, which means that you will be creating a better connection with the other person.

How it works:

No one wants to spend time with a negative person—someone who looks upon life from a "glass half empty" perspective. When you can reframe something for yourself, you will be communicating from a more positive mindset, which will make you a person others want to be with. When you help other people to reframe something, you will make them feel better about themselves, which means that they will want to spend time with you because you make them feel good. Either way, you are building rapport with another person.

Short Real-Life Story about Reframing

Two old friends who haven't seen one another in some time are having lunch and catching up. One has a full-time job in middle management while the other is a marketing consultant who works on a project-by-project basis.

The consultant is lamenting the fact that although he has just had a "very good year," he's winding up the last couple of projects he has under contract and is concerned about how much work he'll have in the year to come.

His friend listens attentively and then exclaims, "Wow, you're really lucky! I envy you!"

"Lucky? Haven't I just told you that I'm not sure what's going to be happening after I finish up these last couple of projects?"

"Yes, absolutely, I hear you," says his friend. "But think about it. You've done well enough so that you don't really have to worry about money for a few months. You still have income coming in from the projects you haven't completed. And it seems like you're actually going to have a little downtime to take care of yourself, refocus, and reenergize so you'll be ready to go full steam ahead when the next project comes along."

By now the consultant is smiling. "You know," he says. "I never thought about it that way. I really have been working very hard. It would be nice to have a little time off. And every time I've been in this position in the past, something's come along when I needed it. Thanks for helping me to look on the bright side. We should get together more often. I always feel better when I'm with you."

Examples of Reframing

Problem	Reframed
It's been raining all week. It's been horrible.	All this rain has been so helpful for the gardens, and it's cleaned the streets.
She drives me crazy with all of her details.	Isn't it nice we have someone who manages all the details? It certainly isn't my thing.
The phone has been busy all day at work.	It's nice knowing that business is booming. You can tell by all these phone calls.
My phone hasn't stopped ringing since I got home from work.	I love knowing that I have such a wide circle of friends.

Future Pacing

What it is:

Future pacing is a way to communicate to another person that whatever he or she may have been anticipating as a negative experience or outcome could very well turn out to be a positive one.

What it does:

When you create an opportunity for someone else to view the future in a more positive light you are, in effect, the bearer of good tidings. This will allow the person with whom you are communicating to see not only him/herself but also you more positively because he or she will be more optimistic.

How it works:

Future pacing "leads" the person with whom you are communicating into the future with positive expectations. It is a particularly effective method to use when you are making a suggestion or giving an instruction to which you think the other person might be resistant. If he or she is led to expect a positive result, that resistance will be diffused, and your communication will be much more readily accepted.

Short Real-Life Story about Future Pacing

A child comes home from school, dreading to do his homework. He keeps saying, "My homework is going to be difficult. I'm not going to be able to do it." His mother asks him, "How do you know? You haven't even started it yet." The child goes on to say that when his teacher assigned the homework she'd told the class, "Don't wait to do your homework until Sunday. Do it on Saturday. It's a difficult assignment, and the last class didn't do very well with it, so plan on working hard and taking some time—you'll need it."

The boy's mother immediately understood that his teacher had influenced him in a negative way by leading him to expect that he would have difficulty completing the assignment.

She also understood that it would probably not be as difficult as he anticipated and that she could easily influence him to change his expectation to one that was more positive. What she told him was, "I see you picking this up very easily. You're good at grasping new information, and you're good at remembering what you've been taught. My hunch is that you will finish this homework easily and quickly and come to me bragging about how easy it was for you."

Sure enough, the boy broke into a smile and went off to begin his homework. Not very long after, he came back beaming. "Boy," he said. "You were really right. The next time someone tries to make me think I can't do something, I'm going to remember what you said about my understanding new information and I'm going to remind myself that you were right."

Examples of Future Pacing

You're about to enter the friendliest city on the West Coast!

You're about to experience the world's best hot dogs!

We're famous for our fast service!

You may experience a slowdown in traffic. We're making improvements on the highway.

Installing

What it is:

Making an intentional suggestion to persuade another person of something without his being aware that this is what you are doing.

What it does:

Installing a suggestion in the mind of another person is a way to create an unconscious connection with that person and to increase your chances of receiving the desired response.

How it works:

Installing works on the level of a subliminal communication. Let's say, for example, that I'm on a radio program and the host asks me a question. I might respond by saying, "You know, that's one of the questions people who come to my seminars ask most frequently." By saying that, I've installed in the minds of the listening audience that they, too, might want to attend one of my seminars, even though they may not have thought about it before—or might not even have known that I give seminars.

Short Real-Life Story about Installing

At a business networking meeting, a Life Coach is socializing with the other people at her table, joining in the conversation while being careful not to come across as being there only to get their business.

Of the four people at her table, three are small-business owners who are experiencing some degree of stress and becoming a bit overwhelmed by trying to balance their business and family life. The Life Coach, who sincerely wants to help, asks if she can tell them a story about a client with a similar problem whom she has been helping. She explains that she was able to give her client a strategy for dealing with his situation that brought immediate positive results. She then goes on to say that now, when she meets with this client each week, the client constantly reminds her how much of a difference the strategy has made in his life.

As the Life Coach is telling them about the strategy, three of the four people at the table are listening intently and taking notes. It's clear that they're interested in trying the strategy the Life Coach recommended to her client.

When she is telling them about how she helped her client, the Life Coach is actually installing (or suggesting) that the people at her table could also profit from her coaching. At the end of the meeting, one of the people at the table indicates that he is interested in working with the Life Coach and asks her to describe what a session might be like.

By being generous with her information and strategies, the Life Coach successfully attracted clients without ever having to directly sell herself or convince anyone to hire her.

Examples of Negative Installing and Positive Installing

Negative Installing	Positive Installing
Don't **trip**.	On our survey, we want to see you check off **Extremely Satisfied** on your evaluation.
Don't get **hurt**.	
Don't **burn** yourself.	Many people **check** my **website daily**.
Beware of Dog	
Slippery When Wet	Like thousands of people, **you'll brag** about our award-winning desserts.
No **Jumping** Off Bridge	

Positive Presupposition

What it is:

To have a positive presupposition about something is to assume that it is possible or that it will happen.

What it does:

If you inject a positive presupposition into a question or other communication, you are making it much more likely that you will receive the response you are looking for.

How it works:

To create a connection with another person, you need to have a dialogue. Injecting a positive presupposition into a question or suggestion makes it much more likely that the other person will respond in a way that opens up the conversation to further dialogue—which means that you'll be creating a connection.

Short Real-Life Story about Presupposition

A new high school teacher began the school year filled with enthusiasm for her job. She decided she would be one of those teachers who inspire and make a difference for their students. She was in for a surprise, however, when she tried to get her teenage students to participate in class by asking them questions like:

Does anybody have a question?
Are there any comments?
Is this clear?
Is there anyone who has an answer?
Does this make sense?

All her well-intentioned questions yielded the same response—blank looks and silence. Frustrated and disappointed, she talked to a well-loved teacher who had an excellent track record for getting his students to participate. Upon hearing his new colleague's problem, the seasoned teacher asked, "Do you suppose there are students in your class who do want to participate or who do have the answer when you ask a question?"

"Yes! I know that there are students who want to participate," she responded at once.

The successful, seasoned teacher then offered to help her reword her questions in a way that implied she assumed someone wanted to answer and/or would have the answer. Here is what he told her she should ask:

> Who would like to go first? (Presupposing that someone does want to go first.)
> My hunch is there are a couple of you who have questions. Who is that? (Presupposing that some do have questions.)
> Who has a comment? (Presupposing that someone does.)
> Who would like to go next? (Presupposing that someone does want to go next.)

As soon as the new teacher started to use these phrases she noticed that her use of positive presuppositions was bringing the results she wanted. Her students were now responding, and a dialogue opened up in the classroom.

Examples of Presuppositions

Example	Presupposition
Learn how to housebreak your puppy in three days.	It's possible in three days.
Learn how to drive traffic to your website with your articles.	It's possible that articles will bring traffic to your website.
Who'd like to go next?	Assumes somebody wants to go next.
Who'd like to go first?	Assumes somebody wants to go first.
Who hasn't shared and would like to?	Assumes that someone who hasn't shared wants to.
Tell me what you like best about this class.	Assumes that somebody liked something about the class.
After you take out the garbage, we'll have dinner.	Presupposes that someone will take out the garbage.
In your enthusiasm to share my book with others . . .	Presupposes that the listener is enthusiastic and is going to share it.

PART VI

MAKING CONNECTIONS IN EVERY ASPECT OF YOUR LIFE

Creating Positive Connections

At home and at work, at school, and in our community, we all spend most of our time in relationships with many different people who have many different styles of communicating. The more positive connections you make with all of these people, the happier and more successful you will be in every area of your life.

In the following pages you will learn how to create and maintain more rapport with each of the four different communication styles in seven of the most common types of relationships:

- Spouses and partners
- Parents and children
- Coaches, counselors, and their clients
- Teachers and their students
- Supervisors and staff
- Salespeople and customers
- Website owners and their visitors

In many of these relationships, there are times when you'll find yourself communicating with a group of people who are almost sure to have different styles. When you're aware of their styles and the methods of communication that appeal to each one, you will be able to connect better with all of them.

You may remember that at the beginning of this book, I said I was incorporating a variety of techniques—ranging from the use of white space, to illustrations, to worksheets, to case studies—designed to appeal to readers of different styles. You can do the same thing when trying to create rapport with a group. For example, you might ask, "Do you see what I mean? Does this sound right to you? How do you feel about it? Does it make sense?" Although the group won't realize it, what you're doing here is asking the same question in four different ways, so that people of different styles will be able to respond to it.

As you become more aware of the words and phrases each style uses and likes to hear, as well as their other likes and dislikes, creating this kind of rapport with a group will become something you do automatically.

Spouses and Partners

There's a 3 in 4 chance that you and your spouse or partner have different communication styles. The better able you are to identify and calibrate the other person's style—and he or she yours—the better able you each will be to express your affection and gratitude for the other in a way that he or she can appreciate.

Use the Communication Styles Self-Assessment Test

After you've taken the test and determined your own communication style, ask your partner or spouse to take it. (Or you can both take it at the same time.) Explain that the goal is for each of you to understand the other person better so that you can maximize the rapport you already have with one another.

Tip for Applying

You can have a lot of fun learning and sharing this information—even teasing one another about your particular styles as a way of acknowledging what you have learned.

Keep your test results posted someplace where you will both see them as a way of reminding yourselves how the other person prefers to communicate.

How Each Style Likes to SHOW Affection

Visual	Gift giving
Auditory	Telling others how they feel about them
Kinesthetic	Touching
Digital	Servicing and doing things for others

How Each Style Likes to RECEIVE Affection

Visual	Receiving gifts
Auditory	Hearing how others feel about them
Kinesthetic	By being touched
Digital	Having others do things for them (example: getting a massage)

How to Show Each Style APPRECIATION and GRATITUDE

Visual	Give a gift. Give money.
Auditory	Say thank you.
Kinesthetic	Write a thank-you card.
Digital	Through service.

How to Present Ideas and Information to Each Style

Visual	Be concise. Give a big picture of the idea (few details). "Paint" a picture with words. Get to the point quickly. Ask them if this "looks" good to them.
Auditory	Get to the point (it's OK to be blunt). Present it as an "idea." Be prepared to have a conversation about it and to hear their ideas. Be prepared to have them want to "improve" or add to your idea. Ask them if this "sounds" like a good idea.
Kinesthetic	Calibrate the correct time to present the idea. Make it fun or lighthearted for them. Ask them if this "feels" like a good idea.
Digital	Present your idea as an adventure for them. Give them plenty of details and options. Give them choices to choose from. Give them time to process and think it through. Ask them what they "think" about the idea.

What to Expect from Each Style When Asking Them to Make a Decision

Visual	Usually makes decisions quickly Does not need lots of details
Auditory	May ask a series of questions and then will make a decision quickly
Kinesthetic	Give them time to "feel it through" Keep it simple—not too many choices
Digital	Give them processing time (sometimes overnight) May be silent as they are thinking it through

Parents and Children

If you are a parent, you know how difficult it can be to communicate and connect with even one child. That problem can then be compounded if you are trying to connect with two or more children whose communication styles may be different from one another's and also different from yours. And finally, if your communication style is different from your spouse's or partner's, you may each have to make different adjustments to create rapport with your kids.

Maybe you've noticed that one of your children always tidies up his room when you ask, while another never seems to remember to take out the trash no matter how many times your remind him. Or perhaps you remember that when Sophie was just six years old, you could ask her to "please put the pieces of the puzzle away and then wash your hands and come into the kitchen for lunch," and she'd do all those things after being told just once. Now Mikey is the same age, and given the same instructions, he will either take so long that you wonder what he could possibly be doing in all that time, or he'll beg you to "help" him or do it "with" him. If any of this sounds familiar, Sophie is probably a Digital Style communicator while Mikey is Kinesthetic.

Once you learn to "speak their language," your communications with children of all styles will almost immediately become less difficult, and your connection with them will improve.

Use the Communication Styles Self-Assessment Test

Knowing your own style will allow you to self-monitor and calibrate your communications to better match those of your child(ren).

If your children are old enough to understand and complete the test, ask them to complete it. Children will find it fun to learn their own communication style and see how it either matches or differs from yours. They may also begin to calibrate their own communications to match your style. To facilitate this, you might "install" the idea that connection is a two-way street.

If your children are not capable of taking the test themselves, you can put yourself in their place and take the test, answering the questions as you believe they would. The better you understand each style, the more accurately you will be able to do this. You can even ask each child whether he or she agrees with your answers.

If you have more than one child, understanding all their styles will allow you to design and employ the methods of communication that create the greatest connection and rapport with each one. And, as a bonus, you will then have the tools to also help children of different styles connect better with one another—so your children will be getting along better with one another.

Tip for Applying

Post the results of your own and each child's test on the refrigerator, kitchen cupboard, or even the bathroom mirror. You can also post the list of each style's commonly used words to remind yourself of how to calibrate your communications.

Words That Will Help You Match Your Child's Communication Style

Visual	See, look, picture, imagine, appear, view
Auditory	Hear, sound, resonate, tell me, harmony, idea
Kinesthetic	Feel, touch, together, comfortable, connect
Digital	Perceive, consider, detail, know, describe, figure out, process, logical

How to Build Rapport with Each Child's Style

Visual	Don't give them too many details.
	Tell them how long they have to complete a task.
	Let them know in advance when something is expected.
	Post lists that they can look at; try using different colored pencils for this.
Auditory	Give them step-by-step instructions.
	Ask them if they "heard" you.
	Ask them to give you their ideas about how to do it "better."
	Remember, longer tasks will cause them to lose their focus and want to move on to something else.
Kinesthetic	Don't give them too many choices.
	Try to present tasks in a fun way.
	Ask if they feel comfortable with what you've proposed.
	Ask how you can support them in completing a task.
	Give them lots of hugs.
Digital	Ask them to do something rather than tell them what to do.
	When you ask them to do something, explain why.
	Prove to them that you trust them; don't keep checking on them.
	Give them sufficient time to complete the task; don't rush them.

Coaches, Counselors, and Their Clients

To be a successful coach or counselor you need to collect information from your client. You need to ask sometimes sensitive and personal questions to find out what your client needs and/or what issues he or she wants to address. If your communication style doesn't match your client's, you are more likely to break rapport because your client doesn't feel heard or believes he or she is being misunderstood. When that happens, the client is likely to end your relationship.

Therefore, to be an effective counselor or coach it's important that you understand how to connect quickly with all four of the communication styles so that you build rapport with your clients.

Use the Communication Styles Self-Assessment Test with Your Clients

You can incorporate the test into your intake interview with new clients.

Later on, as you build rapport and if you think it's appropriate, you might consider discussing the results with your client as a way of explaining why he or she connects better with some people than with others. This can help your client to increase self-awareness.

Tip for Applying

Record each client's communication style on his or her file folder to remind yourself of the best way to communicate with that client during your sessions. You can also record:

- Questions the client will relate and respond to easily
- How best to support or counsel his or her style

You can use the following lists as your guides.

Questions That Will Engage Your Coaching and Counseling Client

Visual	Can you see yourself doing this in the future?
	Does this look like the picture you had in mind?
	Are you clear about your direction?
	What do you see as your next steps?
Auditory	What ideas do you have about your goal?
	What did I say that resonates with you?
	How can you improve upon your idea?
	Any "what if" type questions
Kinesthetic	What can we do together to keep moving forward?
	Which one feels better, A or B?
	How can I best support you?
	Does this fit for you? Is it a match?
Digital	What are your thoughts about this plan?
	Is this direction making sense for you?
	What is your sequence for the next steps?
	What did you like best about this session?

How Best to Support or Counsel Each Communication Style

You will get faster responses and results when you have the ability to coach or counsel your client in a way that matches his or her communication style. Here are some tips and strategies that you can use to support your client, remembering that staying in rapport and maintaining a connection will bring the results you both desire:

Visual	These are the folks who are good at seeing the big picture. Support them in finding a team to help them with the details.
	Book short meetings and adhere to the agreed-upon time frame.
	Ask them for an update on what they've completed since your last meeting.
	They will probably come prepared with a list of accomplishments and check off each item as it's completed.
	They tend to know their vision/goal already.
Auditory	These are problem solvers and idea people, which means that they may keep coming up with new approaches to the same problem or skip from project to project.
	Listen to their NEW ideas and stories. If you don't, they may shut down.
	Help them stay on track and stay focused on the current project.
	Remind them it's OK to have many projects—but this is the one you're focusing on now.
	Acknowledge that you've heard what they have to say. If you don't, they will tend to repeat themselves.

MICHAEL LOSIER

Kinesthetic	This group generally prefers one-on-one, in-person coaching sessions.
	Connection is important to them. Allow time for a bit of personal chat at the start of the session, and share something about yourself.
	These people take their time and often have trouble making decisions. Give them as few choices as possible; having too many choices tends to overwhelm them.
	If they are given homework or an exercise to complete, they will probably want to do it with you or someone else. Encourage them to find a partner they can work with to get their work completed.
	Whenever possible, try to incorporate some "fun" into your sessions.
Digital	These clients may sound like they "know it all"—and they usually do.
	Give them time to prepare their sequence of upcoming tasks or projects.
	These are the folks who love order, processes, and structure.
	Encourage them to come up with a step-by-step plan that works for them.
	Avoid telling them directly what to do.

Teachers and Their Students

If you're a teacher, you may be tired of hearing students complain that they're bored or that they're just "not getting it." The challenge for any teacher is to appeal to students of all communication styles. Their communication styles determine how they prefer to receive and process information—in other words, how they learn. The more you know about how each style likes to learn, the better able you will be to connect with and therefore engage all the students in your classroom. Students who are engaged learn better and retain more of what they've learned.

Use the Communication Styles Self-Assessment Test

If possible, it is extremely useful to have your students complete the test. You can explain that the information it supplies will help you to connect better with them so that you'll both have a more productive and fulfilling classroom experience.

Tip for Applying

Once they've taken the test, write each student's style next to his or her name in your roll book.

Communication Style Characteristics to Keep in Mind

If you are not able to have your students complete the Self-Assessment Test (if, for example, they are very young) you can determine their styles for yourself by becoming familiar with the following characteristics:

Visual	Like to see diagrams and pictures
	Tend to sit up front so they can see everything (when they sit near the back, can be easily distracted)
	Will answer lots of the questions very quickly
Auditory	Like to hear and tell stories
	Tend not to take notes because they remember what they hear
	May give long detailed answers and love to hear themselves talk
	Tend to ask a lot of good questions
Kinesthetic	Learn best through hands-on experience
	Like to be surrounded by all the comforts of home: pillow, sweater, lots of pens and paper for taking notes
	Work well in teams and in groups
Digital	Like questions that make them think
	Usually sit in the back of the room and tend not to participate in class unless they are asked, "What do you think of this?" or "What are your thoughts?"
	Need time to process answers and sometimes come up with great answers—the NEXT day

Teaching Techniques That Stimulate Each Style

Understanding the way each style prefers to receive and process information will allow you to design and employ a variety of teaching techniques that will accommodate and appeal to all types of students.

What Each Style Likes

Visual	Building a list
	Answering questions out loud
	Using fill-in-the-blank worksheets
	Taking notes
	Using colored pens, markers, highlighters
Auditory	Brainstorming ideas
	Storytelling
	Inventing better ways to do things
	Using music or instruments
	Group debates
Kinesthetic	Having hands-on experiences
	Working with a buddy
	Being creative and having fun
	Using worksheets and assessments
Digital	Sorting new content
	Using charts
	Compiling and analyzing data and statistics
	Using worksheets

What Each Style Dislikes

Visual	Memorizing things
	"Playing"—they would rather work than play
	Listening to lectures
	Personal sharing
	Working in groups
Auditory	Being quiet
	Not having the opportunity to talk and/or answer questions
	Extensive note-taking
Kinesthetic	Not having time for fun
	Not having time to connect with others
	Being rushed
	When things end abruptly
Digital	Long written assignments
	Being interrupted in the middle of a sequence
	Incomplete agendas or lessons
	Being rushed
	Being told what to do

Supervisors and Staff

As a supervisor or manager, you need to communicate not only with your staff as a group but also with each member on a one-on-one basis. It only takes one disgruntled staff or team member to spoil the mood or energy in the entire workplace. Employees expect their supervisor to help and support them. An employee who feels misunderstood or unheard will spread his or her negativity to the entire team.

Knowing how to determine and communicate with all four of the communication styles is important for a number of reasons.

As a supervisor, you want to be able to assemble a team that includes all four styles. Why? Because if all the team members were Visual they would talk only about the "big picture" and never address the details or the process. If all team members were Auditory they would "talk about it" forever, jumping from one good idea to another and never getting around to implementing any of them. A totally Kinesthetic team would spend all their time making sure they were connected and having fun. All Digital? They would spend so much time organizing and making lists that the project might never get off the ground.

Once you've assembled your team, you need to communicate effectively with all of them, which means calibrating your approach to fit their individual styles.

To work together, the various team members need to be able to communicate effectively with one another as well as with you, their supervisor.

When addressing the group as a whole, you need to be able to incorporate all four communication styles to ensure that you are connecting with all members of your staff.

Use the Communication Styles Self-Assessment Test

♦ Ask each member of your staff to take the test to determine his or her communication style.

♦ Have the staff members share their results with one another.

♦ Give each staff member a list of the words most commonly used by each of the styles (or post the list in a place where everyone has access to it).

♦ Try to assign individuals tasks that are suited to their particular communication style. Ideally, each style would be assigned tasks that appease that style (see table on the next page).

Suiting the Task to the Staff Member's Style

When an employee is asked to perform a task that is not a natural match for his or her style, it may not be completed, or if it is, it may not be done as well as it could or should be. Procrastination, excuses for not getting work completed, or uninterested employees slow down progress and productivity at the workplace. When you assign the right task to the right communication style, you will have a high-performance, well-connected, and effective team.

Here are some suggestions for the types of tasks that best suit each communication style:

Visual	Building a vision of the big picture
	Running efficient meetings
	Using flip charts at meetings
	Making sure that meetings run on time
Auditory	Providing leadership
	Brainstorming ideas
	Improving the process
	Making sure all is fair
	Finding the words to best describe a project
Kinesthetic	Building the team
	Creating connections among team members through games and exercises
	Organizing team meetings
	Taking notes during meetings
	Taking care of the details
Digital	Planning the steps and sequence of events
	Asking the "what if" analytical questions
	Bringing logic and order to time management

Communicating with Your Staff as a Whole

Most people hate staff meetings because they think they are a waste of valuable time. But sometimes it's important to communicate with your entire staff at once or to gather everyone together to make a decision. If you accommodate and calibrate for the various communication styles of your staff members, you will ensure that your meetings are more productive and less burdensome for everyone— including you.

Visual	Appreciate having an agenda because they value time so much
	Like to know when the meeting will start and especially when it will end
	Prefer meetings that are short (under one hour)
	Will lose focus and stop paying attention more quickly than the other types
	To hold their attention, assign them a task such as making the opening remarks, special announcements, or gathering feedback on the meeting itself
Auditory	Letting them know what subjects will be covered (and what will not be covered) will keep them on track
	Contribute best when they are allowed to voice their opinion or can contribute ideas
	Do well when given a leadership role
Kinesthetic	Appreciate knowing the agenda in advance so that they can "get comfortable" with what's coming up
	Do best in a clean, well-lit, temperature-controlled, comfortable environment
	Are good at note-taking because it keeps them focused and allows them to get a feel for the meeting and project
Digital	Like using an agenda to sequence upcoming events and make sure everything gets covered
	Like being asked to share their opinion; they don't volunteer unless asked
	Will probably be the ones who ask the hard but sometimes necessary questions to ensure that all the steps and processes work

Salespeople and Customers

Anyone who's ever lost a potential sale knows how bad it feels to lose rapport with a customer. Once the connection is broken, it's highly unlikely the sale will be made.

One of the most effective ways to create rapport with a customer is to ask questions that encourage him to reveal his needs. To do that, the salesperson has to ask those questions in a way that will appeal to the customer's communication style.

Use the Communication Styles Self-Assessment Test

The first step toward being able to calibrate another person's style is to be aware of your own. To do that you need to take the Self-Assessment Test. Once you know your own style, you can read about the other three styles so that you'll be able to watch and listen for clues to your customers' preferred means of receiving and processing information and adjust your questions accordingly.

Tip for Applying

Make a list of the characteristics and most commonly used words for each communication style and keep copies at the service counter and next to the telephone to remind you of how to ask the questions that appeal to each style.

How Each Communication Style Tends to Shop

In addition to listening to the customer's choice of words, there are also some common characteristics you can observe to help you uncover your customer's style:

Visual	Tends to make decisions quickly
	Usually does not need the details
	Likes to "look at everything"
	Is influenced by how the product "looks"
Auditory	Likes to talk about his story, why he needs it, what he will do with it, etc.
	Likes new features and gadgets; quality is a key factor
	Asks lots of good questions
	May express interest by using sounds like "ooh, ahhh, hmmm"
	May say the product does or doesn't "resonate" with him
Kinesthetic	Needs to have an enjoyable experience
	The shopping environment needs to "feel" good
	Likes to touch, feel, and hold the product
	Definitely would want to try it on to "see if it fits"
	Likes to be given a "demo"
	Needs time to develop a "gut" feeling to see if it's a match
	Likes to be left alone to make a decision
Digital	Will ask many detailed questions
	Wants facts, statistics, reports, manuals, etc.
	Needs time to process all the information and prefers not to purchase without doing lots of analysis
	Needs time to think it over
	Needs to build trust with the salesperson

Effective Ways to Address Each Communication Style

Visual	Does this one look like what you had in mind?
	Can you see yourself wearing/using this?
	Is this what you pictured?
	It'll just take a minute or two; it will be quick.
	Do you like this look?
	Is this the look you want?
	When you see something you like, let me know.
Auditory	I'll be here when you want to ask me questions.
	Does this sound like what you want?
	Does this resonate with you?
	What do you have in mind?
	What ideas did you have?
Kinesthetic	Does this feel like a match for you?
	Does this feel right/OK?
	Are you comfortable with this?
	Is this a good fit for you?
	Would you like to hold it? Touch it?
	Take your time.
Digital	Do you need some more information to help you decide?
	What else do you need to know?
	Does this make sense?
	Is this the best one for you?
	Does this have all the features you need?
	What do you think of this one? What are you thinking?
	What are your thoughts about this?

Website Owners and Their Visitors

To capture a website visitor and make it more likely that he or she will return often to your site, you need to appeal to the visitor's communication style. If you check the Web traffic results for your site and find that most visitors stay for under two minutes, it's likely that you haven't caught their attention. Each communication style has preferences about what they like to see, read, or hear online. Effective websites appeal to all four communication styles.

Use the Communication Styles Self-Assessment Test

Both you—the website owner—and your website designer should take the Self-Assessment Test to determine your own styles. Then read about the other styles to determine how you can present the information on your site in a way that will have the broadest appeal across all styles.

Tip for Applying

Review each page of your website to see how it appeals to each communication style. Ask family members, colleagues, and friends with different communication styles to visit the site and give you their feedback about what did or did not appeal to them. This will give you insight into whether you have succeeded in connecting with all the different styles.

It's Not Always What IS on Your Website That Matters; It May Be What's NOT

Including elements that appeal to all four communication styles will increase the time that visitors spend on your site.

If you include a Q&A section, for example, you'll be satisfying the Kinesthetic Style's desire for an interactive element and the Digital Style's love of specific information. An introduction allows the Kinesthetic Style to get comfortable with you and the Auditory Style to hear your story, and the option to "skip the introduction" will allow the Visual Style to get right to the point. If the site is easy to navigate (which it should be in any case), it isn't difficult to provide something for everyone while allowing visitors of different styles to skip the elements they don't relate to easily.

What Each Style Likes

Visual	Current photos
	Owner's photo
	Minimal text; bullet points
	Short video clips
Auditory	Sound bites (audio files)
	Proper grammar and spelling
	Stories
Kinesthetic	Welcome message
	Owner's picture to build trust
	Contact information
	Interactive elements
	Ability to post a response
	Ease of navigation
	Video clips
Digital	Q&A section
	Contact information (using a variety of means)
	Facts and figures to support your information

What Each Style Dislikes

Visual	Too much text; not enough graphics
	Lack of owner photo
	Lengthy sales pitch
	Too much animation
	Not neat
Auditory	Poor grammar and syntax
	Too many menus
	Difficulty of navigation; hard to find information
Kinesthetic	Lack of owner photo
	Lack of contact info
	Lengthy sales pitch
Digital	Illogical or unclear tabs
	Lack of organization

PART VII

Ten Special Techniques Teachers and Trainers Can Use to Connect and Accelerate Learning

The Techniques and What They Do

If you are a teacher or trainer, you—more than most people—are likely to be working with people of all four communication styles simultaneously. It is therefore extremely important that you are able to present information in ways that benefit all four styles equally.

The ten techniques I'll be offering here are designed to help you build rapport and increase participation among your students so that they absorb the material faster—that is, at an accelerated speed.

Please note that the use of overhead projectors, flip charts, and other visual aids is not included here. If you do use these tools, I suggest that you do so sparingly, as they are not considered effective for accelerating learning.

The ten techniques are:

1. Asking Enrolling Questions
2. Getting Quick Answers Out Loud
3. Insisting on an Answer
4. "Repeat after Me . . ."
5. Getting Students to Fill In the Blanks
6. "This Is Important—Write It Down"
7. Changing the Energy of the Room
8. Sharing with a Neighbor
9. Sharing in Small Groups
10. Group Recap

Asking Enrolling Questions

What it is:

An enrolling question is one that you ask with the intention of getting a response from a majority of people in the group.

What it does:

- ♦ It lets students know that the class or session is intended to be interactive and that they will all be expected to participate.
- ♦ It breaks down barriers to participation.
- ♦ It gives each student an opportunity to participate.
- ♦ It shows leadership from the teacher or trainer.

How it works:

This is a good technique to use at the beginning of a class or session.

The technique is most effective when the teacher or trainer asks two questions that are intended to elicit positive responses from two different groups of people—as in "Who here likes ice cream?" "Who here does not like ice cream?" This ensures that the majority of students will be participating.

As the trainer asks the first question, he raises his right hand and holds it up so that students will understand they are expected to answer by raising their hands in response. When asking the second question, the trainer holds up his left hand to indicate that this is a new question and that it also requires a response.

MICHAEL LOSIER

Initially, some students may be shy or quiet and not ready to participate. When the teacher or trainer keeps his hand in the air for twenty to thirty seconds, those who are reluctant will be encouraged to respond as they see others participating.

Important Key to This Technique

It is important to ask the questions beginning with the words "Who here . . ." That wording presupposes that someone will answer the question.

Sample Enrolling Questions

Trainer	Two Enrolling Questions, one for each hand
A fitness trainer giving a presentation may ask...	Who here has found they have challenges staying on track with their exercise routine?
	Who here finds it easy to stay on track with their exercise routine?
A life coach giving a presentation may ask...	Who here is finding their life a little hectic and somewhat out of balance?
	Who here knows someone who has a balanced life and is successful in everything he does?
A website designer giving a presentation may ask...	Who here is overwhelmed with all the things they need to get their website up and running?
	Who here has been to an informative and attractive website and is determined to create one that is equally impressive?
A relationship coach giving a presentation may ask...	Who here is having challenges communicating with some clients/customers?
	Who here finds they connect with people really easily?

Getting Quick Answers Out Loud

What it is:

This is a way to format questions so that they elicit a quick one- or two-word answer from everyone in the room.

What it does:

♦ Encourages students to pay attention
♦ Encourages students to participate verbally
♦ Allows students to integrate new information by giving the answer out loud
♦ Helps students to remember what they've learned because they hear it out loud from the entire group
♦ Keeps the energy in the room high

How it works:

When a teacher or trainer provides information in the form of a lecture, students tend to lose interest or lose focus. Asking questions in a way that requires them to give short answers out loud at least every two to three minutes helps them to pay attention and remain engaged. Students also feel that they are really learning when they are able to "get the answer right."

In addition, if someone answers incorrectly, the incorrect answer provides the teacher or trainer with an opportunity to thank the responder for his or her participation and then expand upon the point in question by asking for more input from the group.

Important Key to This Technique

The more the teacher asks for answers, the more students are required to participate. When a teacher or trainer uses

MICHAEL LOSIER

this technique, students often remark upon how quickly the time seems to pass and how easy it is to retain the information.

Sample Questions That Elicit Quick Answers

If a teacher is teaching a young group of students that there are eight sides to an octagon and four sides to a square, the teacher could recap the information by asking:

♦ There are how many sides to an octagon?
All students would reply together "eight."

♦ How many sides to a square?
All students would reply together "four."

Insisting on an Answer

What it is:

Insisting on an answer means that when a teacher or trainer asks a question of the group, he or she does not move on to the next point until receiving a response.

What it does:

♦ Signals the teacher's or trainer's expectations
♦ Encourages students to stay alert and pay attention
♦ Loosens students up and helps break down shyness barriers so that all members of the group are more willing to respond
♦ Sets the tone for a high-participation learning experience

How it works:

If the teacher or trainer asks a question and receives no response, he or she continues to make statements that indicate that the question will not go unanswered.

Important Key to This Technique

When this technique is used very early in the training or teaching session, the teacher or trainer will need to use it only once or twice before students understand that they are expected to answer questions out loud.

Sample "Insisting" Statements

♦ I'll need all of you to answer. Let's try that again.
♦ OK, just a few of you? Let's try that again. Who here . . . ?
♦ I know you may not be in the habit of answering out loud, so let's try that again.

"Repeat after Me . . ."

What it is:

> When a teacher or trainer provides a key piece of information, he or she may ask a question that requires the class to repeat what has just been said.

What it does:

> ♦ Allows students to integrate new information by repeating the answer out loud
> ♦ Helps students remember by hearing the answers spoken out loud by the entire group
> ♦ Keeps the energy in the room high
> ♦ Engages students and keeps them alert
> ♦ Makes students feel they are part of the learning process

How it works:

> When students receive large quantities of information, they may become overloaded and stop listening or participating. If they hear the information only once, they may not remember or recall it. Asking them to repeat it ensures that they stay alert and that they hear it more than once, which means they'll be more likely to remember it.

Important Key to This Technique

> Like Getting Quick Answers Out Loud, this technique should be used at least every two or three minutes in the course of a class or training session.

> Students will learn to answer quickly, and the trainer or teacher will find a high percentage of students participating.

Even shy students and those who tend not to share will catch themselves participating more often.

Sample "Repeat after Me" Statements and Questions

For a fitness trainer giving a presentation	Thirty minutes of cardio is a good standard for daily exercise. How many minutes?
For a website designer giving a seminar	It's helpful to have your Contact Us link on the top right-hand side of the screen on your Web page. So where should the Contact Us link be?
For a teacher giving a geography lesson	There are seven territories in that country. How many territories?

Getting Students to Fill In the Blanks

What it is:

This technique requires the teacher or trainer to come to the class or session with a preprepared worksheet with blank spaces that will require the students or participants to fill in missing information as directed by the teacher.

What it does:

- ♦ Simply having the worksheet in front of them gives the students something to focus on.
- ♦ Once the students realize they will be required to fill in the blanks at regular intervals, they will be more likely to pay attention so that they don't miss anything.
- ♦ Students will want to have all the blanks filled in and will therefore pay attention.

How it works:

Once the participants have filled in their worksheets, they will be more likely to take them home. Having the completed worksheets allows students to revisit their notes as a way to reinforce and refresh their memory.

The worksheet should also supply the teacher's or trainer's website address so that students know where to go for further information.

Important Key to This Technique

Worksheets that include blank lines, boxes, tables, circles, or other creative teaching tools will be the most effective. Teachers should be sure that students will have something to fill in at least every five minutes to ensure that they remain focused.

Examples of How to Use Fill-in-the-Blanks Worksheets

Use statements such as:

♦ Go to line 5 and fill in the name . . .
♦ Go to the box on the top of the page and write . . .
♦ Draw a circle in the middle of the page and in the circle put . . .

"This Is Important—Write It Down"

What it is:

It is a way to be sure that students are paying attention when the teacher or trainer is about to provide an important piece of information.

What it does:

- Alerts daydreaming students to refocus
- Encourages students to participate by writing things down

How it works:

When the teacher or trainer finds the class is "drifting" or "losing focus," this technique will get students to sit up and take notice. It also ensures that important points are not lost and receive the attention they deserve.

Important Key to This Technique

Use this expression sparingly. If you overuse it, students may begin to assume that you think everything is important and will stop taking you seriously.

Examples of "This Is Important" Phrases

- This is important; I'd like you to write it down.
- This is important; make a note of it.
- This is important; you'll need to understand this well.

Changing the Energy in the Room

What it is:

> It is a way for the teacher or trainer to reenergize a group of students who have lost focus and are no longer participating.

What it does:

> It ensures that students will profit from what is being taught because they remain engaged in what the teacher is saying.

How it works:

> When a teacher or trainer does something different, or asks the students to do something different or unexpected, the energy in the room is revitalized and students who may have been bored or losing focus will be more likely to reconnect with the teacher and the material.

Important Key to This Technique

> Don't wait too long before you use this technique. As soon as you sense that the students' energy is flagging or the room is becoming too quiet, do something to "shake things up" and "get the cobwebs out."

Examples of How to Change the Energy of the Room

- Have the students stand up and stretch.
- Encourage the students to applaud after someone gives an answer.
- Change your own position on the podium or at the front of the room. Stand in one place when telling a story, then move to another place when asking a question. Change your position when you change the subject.

Sharing with a Neighbor

What it is:

It's a way to get students to interact with one another in the classroom.

What it does:

♦ Helps students break the ice
♦ Gets even shy students excited about sharing their thoughts
♦ Raises the energy and mood in the room
♦ Ensures that students are integrating the information by discussing it
♦ Gives students the opportunity to have a voice during the training or class
♦ Gives information added value for students because they have received it from a peer rather than the teacher

How it works:

Ask the students to turn to the person on their left (or right) and comment on the information they've just received. Giving students this opportunity is a way to help them digest and integrate what they've just learned. While students are sharing, the teacher or trainer can take a few moments to prepare the next point to be presented.

Important Key to This Technique

Keep the sharing time to one or two minutes and be sure that all students participate. Do this exercise at least once during the training session or class.

Examples of How to Ask Students to Share

- ◆ Please turn to the person on your left, and each of you take one minute to share your opinion of what we just discussed.
- ◆ Please turn to your neighbor and give him the top three [fill in the blank] you've learned from what we just discussed.
- ◆ In under two minutes, please share your experience of the last exercise with the person on your right.

Sharing in Small Groups

What it is:

Three to five people form a small group to discuss the topic of the session or class.

What it does:

- Students integrate the information as they share it with others.
- Students will feel empowered as they share and learn with others in the group.
- Hearing what others have to say heightens the learning experience for all.
- The trainer or teacher will see and hear how well the students have engaged in and learned the information being taught.

How it works:

Ask the students or trainees to break into groups of three to five people. If the seats in the room are moveable, they can pull their chairs into a circle to do this. Restate the topic and explain that this is an opportunity for members of each group to discuss what they've taken from the material just presented. During the group discussion the teacher or trainer will have the opportunity to review and prepare for the next segment of his or her presentation.

Important Key to This Technique

Give clear instructions that each person in the group is to take three or four (or more) minutes to share his or her thoughts. Make it clear that you expect all members of every group to participate.

Appoint a timekeeper in each group to ensure that students stay within their time limit.

Example of How to Present This Technique

Say, "I'd like you to form groups of four (or more) people. Each person in the group will have two minutes to share his or her comments on [fill in the blank] with the other members of the group. We will begin in one minute."

Group Recap

What it is:

This is an energizing, fun way to get students to repeat key points of the lesson out loud so that they are more likely to remember what they've just learned.

What it does:

- ♦ Empowers students who realize how much they have learned by repeating key points out loud
- ♦ Creates good energy at the close of the lesson or session
- ♦ Helps students to integrate new information
- ♦ Provides another opportunity for students to hear points they may have missed the first time

How it works:

The teacher or trainer provides the "lead-in" to each key piece of information and, as he or she reaches the key point, raises both hands, palms up, in the classic questioning position, thus inviting the students to "fill in the blank" out loud, in unison.

Important Key to This Technique

The teacher or trainer needs to determine in advance how many minutes he or she will need for the group recap and time the rest of the lesson or session accordingly. This technique can also be used partway through a lesson or session before moving on to a new subject.

Example of How to Initiate and Facilitate a Group Recap

Say, "Everyone please close your books and put away your papers. When I raise both hands like this (demonstrate palms-up position) it means that I want you all to fill in the next piece of information. Let's begin."

As they raise their hands, teachers and trainers should also indicate by their tone of voice that there is a blank to be filled in and try to adopt a questioning facial expression. Keep hands raised as you wait for the class to respond.

Applying This Book to YOUR Life

It is likely that within the next few days—or even sooner—you will start to become aware of the words most commonly used by your family, friends, and colleagues. You will also catch yourself using the words that are common to your own communication style. Noticing these words in yourself and others means that you are integrating and implementing the material you have just learned.

You may also notice your calibration skills improve as you become more aware of checking in with others and adjusting your own communication style to the mood and style of another person or a group of people.

The increased speed at which you connect with others will become evident as you continue to build rapport by calibrating and noticing how others communicate.

You now have all the knowledge and tools you need to maximize your communication skills.

Apply what you've learned from this book with your spouse or partner, your extended family, your friends, and at your workplace.

Share this book with others and help them to form better connections with you and with everyone in their lives.

About the Author

Michael J. Losier (Low-zee-eh) lives in beautiful Victoria, BC, on Canada's west coast. He is a Neuro-Linguistic Programming (NLP) practitioner and the author of *Law of Attraction: The Science of Attracting More of What You Want and Less of What You Don't*, which has to date sold more than 250,000 copies and is now published in twenty-eight languages throughout the world.

He has also certified hundreds of Law of Attraction Facilitators, teaching them how to communicate their message while stimulating high participation from their students.

Since 1999, Michael has completed more than 1,700 hours of teleclasses, hundreds of one-on-one Law of Attraction coaching sessions, and more than one thousand live training sessions on the Law of Attraction.

A sought-after, dynamic speaker and seminar leader, Michael uses NLP techniques to wow his audiences while teaching them in a way that increases retention of what they learn.

For more information about this book, go to www.LawofConnectionBook.com.

For more information about *Law of Attraction*, go to www.LawofAttractionBook.com.